7/04

Gun Dogs

Playful Pup to Hunting Partner

by John R. Falk

Voyageur Press

Edited by Todd R. Berger
Designed by Leslie Ross

Printed in China

First hardcover edition
00   01   02   03   04   6   5   4   3   2

First softcover edition
03   04   05   06   07   5   4   3   2   1

Library of Congress Cataloging-in-Publication Data
Falk, John R.
    Gun dogs / by John R. Falk.
        p.   cm. — (Master training series)
    Includes bibliographical references and index.
    ISBN 0-89658-343-0
    ISBN 0-89658-004-0(pbk.)
    1. Hunting dogs–Training. I. Title. II. Series.
SF428.5.F345   1997   96-42375
636.7'52—dc20   CIP

Published by Voyageur Press, Inc.
123 North Second Street, P.O. Box 338, Stillwater, MN 55082 U.S.A.
651-430-2210, fax 651-430-2211
books@voyageurpress.com
www.voyageurpress.com

Educators, fundraisers, premium and gift buyers, publicists, and marketing man-agers: Looking for creative products and new sales ideas? Voyageur Press books are available at special discounts when purchased in quantities, and special editions can be created to your specifications. For details contact the marketing department at 800-888-9653.

Front Cover Photo © Alan and Sandy Carey
Back Cover Photo © William H. Mullins
Title Page Photo © Alan and Sandy Carey
Photo Page 4 © Denver Bryan

Acknowledgments

It gives one pause when first considering where to begin the thanks due for the successful completion of a project, especially one like this book. Seldom the work of only its author, a finished book always represents an amalgam of effort by numerous persons. In support of the author are publisher, editors, photographers, production folk, and, ultimately, marketing and sales personnel. Each is a value-added contributor. So, logically, that's where my thanks begins, herewith sincerely extended to all of them.

Further, though, a book is the sum of its author: the experiences, the people, friends, family, other writers—and in the case of this book, the gun dogs, themselves—that make up that total. But, rather than including a litany of names, and accidentally slighting someone, I shall simply say thanks to all of you . . . and God bless!

Dedication

To those wonderful, patient women—my Mother (God rest her soul) and my sweet wife—without whose love and understanding of my incurable addiction to dogs in general, and to gun dogs in particular, would have denied me the satisfying enrichment provided by dozens of memorable canine companions through the years. That both ladies happened to be pushovers for cute pups and, later, big brown eyes and proffered paws only added icing to the cake.

Contents

A Dog's Prayer

Treat me kindly, my Beloved Master, for no heart in all the world is more grateful for kindness than the loving heart of me.

Do not break my spirit with a stick, for though I should lick your hand between blows, your patience and understanding will more quickly teach me things you would have me know.

Speak to me often, for your voice is the world's sweetest music, as you must know by the fierce wagging of my tail when your footsteps fall upon by waiting ears.

When it is cold and wet, please take me inside, for I am no longer used to the bitter elements and I ask no greater glory than the privilege of sitting at your feet beside the hearth. Though you had no home, I would rather follow you through ice and snow than rest on the softest pillow in the warmest home.

Keep my pan filled with fresh water for although I should not reproach you were it dry, I cannot tell you when I suffer thirst. Feed me clean food, that I may stand well, to romp and play and do your bidding, to walk by your side, and stand ready, willing, and able to protect you with my life, should your life be in danger.

Then, my Beloved Master, should the Great Master seek to deprive me of my health and spirit, do not turn me away. Rather, hold me gently in your arms as merciful sleep is administered, and I will leave you knowing with the last breath I draw, my fate was ever safest in your hands.

Author Unknown

About the Book

Gun Dogs, the first book in the Master Training Series, will be most beneficial for three categories of hunters: those who would like to be gun dog owners; those about to take the plunge and buy a gun dog; and those already in their freshman, sophomore, or junior years as owners. It is fair to say that all three groups occupy a learning niche, earnestly prospecting for every gem of information about the fascinating realm of gun dogs.

This book strives to motivate the would-bes, to assist the plungees, and to nourish the inductees. You will find here an abundance of gun dog training instruction, advice, and opinion, helpful to many, provocative to some, and, hopefully, interesting to all.

Taking pleasure to new heights, this brace of English setters makes a high-country chukar hunt a memorable day for their owner. Photo © William H. Mullins

Introduction

It is increasingly obvious that our growing population is eroding what were once seemingly limitless outdoor horizons. Vast tracts of unspoiled open land, shriveling now to postage-stamp proportions in too many places under the inexorable march of progress, no longer provide the inexhaustable crop of consumable wildlife our ancestors enjoyed and probably took for granted.

Rightly, it's been said that we must wring out every possible ounce of satisfaction from the outdoor experience. With fewer fish to catch, we eschew taking a limit, turning some back as "too valuable to catch only once" as Lee Wulff advocated. As hunters, we cannot fulfill the experience of the chase without the kill; but if we could, at least a portion of our bag would willingly be returned to the coverts, so that we, or someone else, could again share in enjoying it another day.

Even though we lack yesterday's ample supply of game and easily accessible, uncrowded hunting venues, we still must content ourselves with what *is* available. In addition to thanking the Almighty, we extend our gratitude to those "Best Friends," whose unfailing companionship and gratifying performance so enrich our days afield. How better to magnify the moments, to extract the greatest pleasure from the outdoors experience, than with those very special partners we call gun dogs?

The start or end of a perfect day afield? Either way, the investment in a gun dog is what makes it worthwhile. Photo © Bill Buckley/The Green Agency

Is a Gun Dog Worth the Investment?

At the outset of a book on gun dogs, it might strike some readers as impolitic to question the wisdom of investing in a gun dog. After all, it might prove self-defeating to look too deeply into the financial side of the equation instead of letting sleeping dogs lie, as it were. But, since there are two sides to every story—and platitudes and pragmatic-minded spouses should never be scorned—appraising the investment is a necessary exercise.

In the field, the average gun dog offers an alarmingly small return on investment. Consider the length of the open season on game ordinarily hunted with dogs. Typically, waterfowling has about fifty days of legal hunting, bobwhite quail gunning has perhaps ninety, ring-necked pheasant hunting has around forty, ruffed grouse has approximately 100, and roughly forty days are allowed for chasing woodcock.

Even factoring in geographical differences, the potential use of a gun dog during the open hunting season totals only about ten weeks annually. Toss in an extra two weeks to cover any margin of error and the count swells to twelve weeks—a mere quarter of the year.

Exactly where does that leave us during the remaining forty weeks? While contributing no useful hunting work for 75 percent of the year, the gun dog's maintenance costs continue without interruption. There's the annual dog license; the daily dog food; and regular veterinary bills for vaccinations (to prevent parvo, leptospirosis, hepatitis, distemper, Lyme disease, and rabies), in addition to regular wormings, and for medications to guard against heartworm.

Moreover, there are substantial outlays for accessory items—all of which are indispensable for proper canine care and maintenance—such as collars, leads, brushes, a variety of combs, nail clippers, electric hair clippers, food and water bowls, dog beds, and car crates. And don't for-

Unrestrained affection highlights the typical gun dog's appeal to owner and family. This black Lab pup is about to plant a tongue-slosh on an expectant duck hunter's chin. Photo © William H. Mullins

get to count in training- and hunting-related items such as check cords, retrieving dummies, whistles, dog bells and/or beepers, dog boots, blank cartridge guns, and blank ammo.

Additionally, for bird dog or retriever owners there may well be supplementary needs like live pigeons or bobwhite quail to enhance training exercises. Such birds must, of course, be housed and fed, further escalating expenses.

Naturally, before even totaling up all those ancillary expenditures, there's the initial cost of the gun dog itself to consider.

As an investment, gun dogs don't offer much to argue about, even without trying to tally their approximate cost. Owning a gun dog just ain't about to put you on the Fortune 500 list, but that two-sided story mentioned earlier, still has another side.

Let's talk about the gun dog's nine months of supposedly unproductive value. Though the relatively brief open game seasons may shrivel a gun dog's active field work, that doesn't mean putting him on the shelf till next year. Increasingly, with their six-month seasons, public hunting preserves are taking up the slack and adding several months to the gun dog's active field work.

Factor in participation in field trials, and still more weeks can be added to that activity schedule. Suddenly, that miserly quarter of a year mushrooms into a potential eight or nine months of useful gun dog field value. Moreover, the average hunting breed certainly qualifies as an extremely good and valuable family house pet. The exceedingly gentle nature of gun dogs and unabashed displays of affection have always endeared them to families.

And just like any other kind of house dog worthy of the name, the gun dog also renders functional service throughout the year. He serves variously as security patrol, burglar alarm, smoke detector, alarm clock backup, babysitter, and official welcoming committee for visiting friends and returning family members. The gun dog embodies all the exemplary qualities of the family dog.

In addition, the gun dog adds another dimension to his value—he hunts *with* and *for* you every autumn. Try placing a dollar value on the pulse-quickening spectacle of a galloping pointer colliding in midstride with an invisible wall of hot scent, or the water-slamming abandon of a spirited retriever targeting a wing-tipped mallard on a misty woodland pond.

What's his worth? What is the value of the gun dog—ever faithful and affectionate—that speechless friend who gives so much and seeks so little in return? He's the bridge between you and the fauna you hunt. He's the medium that ties you and your quarry most closely together, physically and—infinitely more meaningful—spiritually, creating an enduring respect both for the prey and the hunt, one that only grows deeper with time.

Should you measure a gun dog's worth in investment dollars? To me, the answer is no. If you agree, please read on and enjoy.

Waterfowl-fetching specialists, retrievers, like this black Lab with mallard drake, often do double duty flushing birds in the uplands. Photo © Denver Bryan

The Principal Gun Dog Breeds

RETRIEVERS

Originally, the retriever's job, unlike that of other hunting breeds, didn't begin until the quarry was *downed*, either by arrow or shotgun. Then, after marking the fall, he would run or swim to the spot on command, scoop up the prize, and, with tender mouth, swiftly fetch it to hand.

Primarily waterfowl specialists, retrievers in recent years have found increasing utility as pinch-hit flushing dogs for upland bird hunting.

The Labrador Retriever

As a breed, the Labrador retriever is an embarrassment—an embarrassment of riches, that is. The Labrador retriever inches close to perfection in so many different categories. The Lab, as he's affectionately known to his legions of admirers, is not only the most popular hunting dog breed in America, he is also the most popular *dog*. The Labrador boasts impressive credentials in an equally impressive array of endeavors.

The Lab overwhelmingly dominates retriever field trials; he is one of a select few breeds used as a guide dog for the blind; he serves effectively in law enforcement and customs duties, sniffing out illegal substances and contraband; he locates people buried in collapsed buildings; and he acts as a service dog to the deaf, alerting owners to the ring of the telephone and doorbells.

The Lab combines high trainability with a stable disposition. Such are the essential ingredients that enable him to successfully fill so many varied roles. He brings these same qualities to the waterfowl blind, the field, and the home. Wearing the robes and trappings of "King of Retrievers," the Labrador has earned the right to be the standard bearer for all retriever breeds.

Despite his enormous versatility, the Labrador of hunting lineage is, and was developed as, a retrieving specialist. Please take note of the key words *hunting lineage*. Because of the breed's soaring popularity, not just any Lab can qualify as a hunting Lab. Like many sporting breeds in the United States, Canada, and Britain, the Labrador has been victimized by his own popularity.

The price has been a costly one. The demand for puppies has driven many breeders toward quantity, often at the expense of quality, including a total disregard of hunting characteristics. Add the divisive factor of breeding solely for the show ring, and literally two distinct types of Labradors have resulted, one for bench (show), and one for field.

Belying his origin, the Labrador's lineage reaches to the Canadian province of Newfoundland, of which Labrador is a part. The St. John's Newfoundland, a breed somewhat smaller than its close Newfoundland relative, is said to be the progenitor of the Labrador. Though waterfowl retrieving was originally something of a sideline, the St. John's dogs were nevertheless strongly entrenched in the fetching business, retrieving fish dropped from hoisted nets and carrying ropes between boats and to and from shore.

Turning up in England around 1820, the St. John's dogs rapidly gained favor—with the endorsement of the second Earl of Malmesbury (an influential sportsman of the time)—for their swimming and retrieving abilities. The Earl and Colonel Hawker, another noted British sportsman, both continually referred to the breed as "Labrador" retrievers, and must be credited—or blamed—for the misnomer that persists today.

Although crossbred with various British retriever breeds of the period, the Labrador's strong points prevailed and eventually made producing a consistently uniform breed type possible. In 1903, the Labrador received official recognition by the English Kennel Club and soon made the trek, in limited numbers, back to North America.

The trickle swelled shortly after formation of the Labrador Retriever Club in 1931, followed that same year by the first licensed Labrador field trial in America, in Chester, New York. Blessed with the support of such prestigious boosters as J. F. Carlisle of Wingan Kennels and W. Averell Harriman of Arden Kennels, a financier who later served as ambassador to the Soviet Union and governor of New York, the Lab soon embarked on an unstoppable ride to prominence.

No other breed has acquired as many placements in American re-

In a foggy morning fetch, this Lab slogs through a spread of mostly pintail decoys to bring back a mallard. Photo © Jack Macfarlane

triever field trials. In fact, the wins of all other breeds combined can't match the Lab's total. Nor is it likely that any fetch dogs—other Labradors included—can ever equal the records set by just four super Labrador retrievers: Shed of Arden, Nilo's King Buck, Spirit Lake Duke, and Candlewoods Tanks A Lot—the only multiple winners of the National Retriever Championship.

Yet, it's really as a hunting partner that the breed has scored its most significant wins. A strong, intuitive swimmer with an inherent love of getting soaking wet, the Lab—and remember, we're talking of those from hunting ancestry—takes to retrieving as instinctively as a hen takes to laying eggs.

With a little encouragement—and oftentimes without—most Lab puppies will begin carrying things, even when engaged in other activities. Teaching them to fetch to hand usually follows quickly, beginning with simple play sessions and later extending to formal field and water exercises.

Black and yellow are dominant coat colors of the Labrador retriever. Chocolate is the third acceptable color for the breed. Photo © Bruce Montagne

This high trainability factor blends so naturally with the Lab's balanced temperament, intelligence, and eagerness to learn that practically anyone can successfully guide his schooling. And if the label "workaholic" can be applied to a dog, it aptly fits the Lab. Like the most successful business tycoon, the Lab thrives on a steady diet of work, forever seeking to feed a seemingly insatiable appetite for fetching.

More in keeping with the extra hunting opportunities the Lab affords than for satisfying the breed's work ethic, Lab owners have increasingly used their animals as pinch-hit upland flushing dogs. Pheasants, grouse, woodcock—in short, any upland game bird normally hunted with spaniels—can be worked productively by the breed. And while seldom approaching the spaniel's natural aptitude or style, given proper encouragement and opportunities, most Labs will help put birds in the bag.

Of fairly generous proportions, dogs (the proper name for a male of any breed) measure about 22½ to 24½ inches (57–62 cm) at the shoulder and weigh from 60 to 75 pounds (27–34 kg), while bitches shave an inch or two (3–5 cm) and about five pounds (2 kg) off dogs' stats. Despite their relatively large size, Labs do nicely in the house as companions for the family. But where space or other considerations dictate, they also adapt well to life in a backyard kennel.

A dense, woolly undercoat hides beneath the Labrador's short outer layer and is the underlying (the pun's intended) reason the breed can withstand cold weather and sustained swims in bone-chilling water. His coat comes in three basic colors; black, the most common; yellow, which shades from fox-red to near-white; and chocolate. A cinch to groom, that short coat also sloughs off burrs, beggar's lice, and stickers almost like water off a duck's back. Completing the Lab's pleasing appearance is a full-length, round tail, which is thick and otterlike at the base and tapers gracefully toward its tip.

The Labrador Club of America, a member club of the American Kennel Club (AKC), officially sponsors the breed in the United States. All show specimens and some working Labs are registered with the AKC. However, a majority of hunting Labs are registered with the United Kennel Club. In addition, a few are registered with the *Field Dog Stud Book* of the American Field Publishing Company, a purebred dog registry organization founded primarily for the registration of field bred sporting dogs rather than show bloodlines.

Labrador retrievers of both types, show or field, make great companions, given their gentle nature. It must be repeated, however, that if you want a real hunting partner, make certain the Lab you buy comes from solid, proven hunting stock.

The Golden Retriever

Aptly named, this retriever is the "Golden Boy" of fetch dog breeds. As a working retriever and field-trial competitor, he is firmly in second place behind the Labrador. Unfortunately, he has also fallen prey to the scourge of popularity, becoming the darling of show fanciers and pet breeders.

Whereas the Lab has suffered but two dividing factions, the golden has split into twice that many: field, show, pet, and obedience types. Such divisions dilute the breed's true character and uniformity. Finding a hunting retriever among the numerous goldens bred and sold today is only a bit easier than spotting an alligator in Nome.

A golden from hunting stock is a good water dog with a strong retrieving instinct that will develop steadily with encouragement. Though a slower learner than the Lab, the golden retains his lessons longer with

Golden retrievers from hunting lineage make good water dogs for duck hunting and excellent pinch-hit flushers for upland work. Photo © Denver Bryan

fewer refreshers. And, while the Lab will work for anyone, not so the golden. He begs the close personal attachment of a patient teacher, one with a deft, light touch to bring out his best, which, once earned, is never held back.

Though second fiddle to the Lab in popularity and field-trial accomplishment, the golden is superior as a flushing dog in the uplands. In scenting prowess, he excels over all other fetch breeds, presumably owing, in part, to an Irish setter outcross in his early development.

The first members of the breed touched U.S. soil around 1912, but the golden did not receive recognition by the American Kennel Club until 1932. A half-dozen years passed before establishment of the Golden Retriever Club of America, official sponsor of the breed in the United States.

A scant year later, Paul Blakewell III's Rip became the first golden to win the Field Trial Championship in the United States. After another golden, King Midas of Woodend, won the first National Retriever Championship in 1941, the breed's popularity began to snowball.

In size, the golden approximates the Labrador's height and weight.

Ranging from a light golden to a reddish-golden color, the golden's longhaired coat and leg and tail feathering contribute to his graceful good looks. But, like all longhaired breeds, the golden attracts burrs, twigs, and other field debris.

Normally gentle, genial, and affectionate, the golden does best living indoors where he can share his love, loyalty, and devotion with his owner and family.

The Chesapeake Bay Retriever

Beyond a shadow of a doubt, the Chesapeake Bay retriever qualifies as the greatest water dog in the world. One of only three fetch-dog breeds originated and developed exclusively in the United States, the Chessy is all business when it comes to waterfowling. The product of the early market gunners of Chesapeake Bay, who made their living hunting and shooting game birds and waterfowl for sale to commercial markets, the breed was generated to work, undaunted by rough water or frigid weather, from dawn till dusk, day in and day out. He was also charged with protecting—fiercely, if need be—the day's bag, gear, and, sometimes, his master.

A very distant third in popularity to the Labrador and golden, the Chessy also seldom bests either in field-trial competition. But, for the serious duck and goose hunter, there is no better choice for sheer rugged stamina, determination, and ability. And although sometimes used as an upland flush dog, as a flusher, the Chessy leaves a lot to be desired. This is probably due to being less maneuverable than Labs or goldens for close-cover work and not as kindly inclined toward directional control.

Whereas the top two retriever breeds count versatility as virtues, the Chessy's honest, straightforward specialty is the water retrieve. The Chessy is usually a challenge to train formally for that job, and the breed responds best to kindness and praise, rather than gruff tactics. The Chessy seems to rely more on his own instincts, believing he knows the business of fetching ducks far better than the competition. And he may be right, especially when retrieving crippled ducks in icy, wind-whipped waters.

The Chessy's secret weapon against the elements is a dead-grass-colored, doubly thick, somewhat oily coat, which when wet has a less-than-subtle odor. This, coupled with the breed's average 65 to 75 pounds

(30–34 kg) and height of 25 to 26 inches (64–66 cm) at the shoulder, generally mitigates against house-pet status for him.

Formed in 1918, the American Chesapeake Club is the official sponsoring organization of the breed in the United States.

The American Water Spaniel

The American water spaniel is living proof that good things do come in small packages. Scaling an average weight between 25 and 40 pounds (11–18 kg) and standing 15 to 18 inches (38–46 cm) at the shoulder, the American is the smallest member of the fetch-dog set. For many gunners, the American's small size is a big plus. The breed easily fits into almost any car, house, or kennel. The second of the three retriever breeds originally born and raised in the United States. (the third is the Boykin spaniel), this little guy is versatility incarnate.

Although really a spaniel, the American water spaniel originated as a retriever in the Midwest. An adept swimmer with an innate addiction to water, the American is up to any reasonable fetching task, exempting, perhaps, oversized geese, which he'll gamely attempt to bring back anyway. And after an early-morning duck shoot, the American will eagerly hunt the rest of the lowlands for rails and jacksnipe, flushing his game in the same fashion as any skilled spaniel. Then, without even thinking of an afternoon off, he's ready to scour the uplands for cottontails, hares, grouse, woodcock, or pheasants.

The American wears a dense, wavy or curly coat of liver or dark chocolate color, an effective shield against cold water, inclement weather, and punishing cover. The same thick coat covers and protects his full-length tail.

Typically spaniel in temperament, the American asks for and freely gives affection, continually striving to gain the approval and praise of his owner and family. Like most spaniels, if treated harshly, his sulky side quickly submerges his normally happy attitude. Yet, when treated with kind firmness and measured vocal correction, there are few trainees quicker at learning and retaining their lessons.

Formed in 1881, the American Water Spaniel Club of America is

A favorite of the serious waterfowl gunner, the Chesapeake Bay retriever is uncontested for stamina and determination under the roughest conditions. Photo © Lon E. Lauber

Versatility personified, the plucky little American water spaniel will perform serviceably in hunting virtually anything of reasonable size in feathers or fur. Photo © Dale C. Spartas/The Green Agency

the official sponsor of the breed in the United States. In addition to registration in the American Kennel Club, the American water spaniel is also accepted by the United Kennel Club and the American Field's *Field Dog Stud Book.*

The Irish Water Spaniel
Another spaniel flying under the banner of retriever colors, the Irish water spaniel qualifies quite well, being a waterholic swimmer of superior ability and endurance. Like the Chesapeake, the Irishman seldom shirks from long, arduous fetching assignments under the sorriest weather and water conditions. Such qualities made him a favorite of Midwest market hunters in the 1870s and 1880s, when Labs and goldens were unknown in that part of the country.

In fact, the Irish reigned as the undisputed retriever of choice well into the twentieth century, waning in registration numbers only when the flashier new kids on the block gained initial prominence. Possibly, the Irish's less-manifested talent for work in the uplands was also partly responsible for his dimming popularity. He can and does deliver ser-

Rarer now than other fetch breeds, the Irish water spaniel was once the choice of U.S. market hunters. Photo © Tara Darling

viceable upland hunting performance, however, if training begins early enough for that extra job.

Like the American water spaniel, the Irish has a temperament that reflects his spaniel heritage; a gruff approach to training simply doesn't succeed. Rather, a temperate, but firmly persuasive technique generally elicits the most cooperative behavior. And though the Irish's development is less rapid than most other retriever breeds, his keen intelligence makes him a quick and retentive learner. Standoffish with strangers, the breed loves and needs close family ties, so much so that a kennel existence is definitely not recommended.

The Irishman's distinguishing characteristics are a chocolate-colored coat of tight curls over a dense protective undercoat; a topknot (a crest of hair on the crown of the head); and a virtually hairless, full-length tail. Dogs weigh in at 55 to 65 pounds (25–30 kg) with a shoulder height of 22 to 24 inches (56–61 cm); bitches scale from 7 to 10 pounds (3–5.5 kg) lighter, and stand an inch or two (2.5–5 cm) shorter.

Founded in 1937, the Irish Water Spaniel Club of America is the breed's official sponsor in the United States.

Raucous cackle and clatter of wings mark a cock pheasant's hasty exit from cover, aggressively flushed by a hard hunting springer. Photo © Alan and Sandy Carey

Flushing Dogs

Working diligently in front of the gun, the spaniel seeks out upland birds by means of body and foot scent. Once he finds a bird, he bores in aggressively to flush it from cover, always within gun range, to offer the hunter a fair shot. Then, like the retrievers, he marks the fall and, when ordered, retrieves with a prompt, gentle carry to the gun.

The Springer Spaniel

Americans have always been fascinated with anything labeled "all purpose." Slap that tag onto any merchandise, be it a "one-size-fits-all" cap, a spinning rod "for all freshwater angling," or a sport shirt "for any occasion," and sales boom. Certainly, hunters have never proved immune to the syndrome, forever seeking equipment that "does it all."

But despite a spate of items declared to be "all-purpose," genuine versatility is hard to come by. However, if a gun dog is the object of your search, the springer spaniel epitomizes practical versatility.

Should your gunning interests center on feathered and furred small game in the uplands and early-season ducks in the lowlands, the springer will perform admirably for you. And no better pheasant-hunting breed exists; as the mongoose is to the cobra, the springer is to the ringneck. The springer is, simply, the best breed for pheasant hunting.

The springer, like all flushing dogs, originated in Europe to spring or flush small game and birds from cover, making them fair targets for the hunting hawks and falcons used by the gentry during the Middle Ages. In the late 1500's, Dr. John Caius (pronounced "keys"), a British dog authority, authored *Of Englishe Dogges*, a book in which he distinguished two varieties of spaniels: land and water dogs. The land spaniels were later subdivided into "springers," dogs that sprang or flushed game for sight hounds or hunting hawks, and "setting spaniels," that pointed or "set" game to be ensnared in nets. It is widely conceded that the latter type formed the foundation stock from which today's setter breeds evolved.

Substantially differing in size, the flushing land spaniels routinely took their names from the game they specialized in hunting. Smaller flushing dogs, used primarily as "cocking dogs" for hunting woodcock, acquired the title of "cocker" spaniels, whereas the larger dogs retained the "springer" name.

The bird of prey employed for the chase determined the early spaniel's hunting range. With falcons, which were customarily lofted before loosing the spaniels, the dogs could range freely. When paired with hawks, which took off directly from the hunter's wrist at the quarry's flush, the spaniels had to hunt close.

As firearms came into general use, the spaniel's field style experienced considerable refinement, including a shortened range and the addition of retrieving. Today's springers preserve those traditional advantages in serving the gun.

Through virtually perpetual motion in the uplands, the springer radiates a singular effervescence that mirrors his unrestrained enthusiasm for field work. To be effective for the gun, his consistent quartering pattern—a continuous sweeping back and forth likened to a wiper blade—must keep him within normal shotgun range, never exceeding 30 to 35 yards (27–32 m). With such little latitude in range, the springer achieves most success in hunting close-cover game birds such as ruffed grouse, woodcock, and ringnecked pheasants.

Initially picking up a bird's foot scent, the springer's keen nose un-

Admirably qualified for the role of versatile upland flush dog and retriever, the springer spaniel also serves well for early and mid-season duck-fetching chores. Photo © Alan and Sandy Carey

ravels even a difficult trail, and, finally, whiffing pungent body scent, hones in on his quarry. Then, with vibrating stub tail ablur signaling his assault, he'll relentlessly bore into the cover to push the luckless bird skyward.

At the flush, the well-trained springer will instantly HUP (plop his fanny down) and, if the bird is dropped, await the gun's order to fetch. Seldom will even the biggest ringnecked rooster deter the springer from executing a successful retrieve to hand.

The average field-bred springer takes to retrieving naturally and, given practice, soon acquires skill at marking the fall of a bird. However, a gunner who demands perfection in the hunting field or one who has field-trial ambitions will undoubtedly want his springer force-trained to retrieve.

Part of the springer's field-performance appeal derives from his intense determination. In cover so intimidating that some breeds would barely skirt its edges, the average springer unswervingly plows on through when tracking hot scent. Any game bird that can outmaneuver the springer's combined tenacity and aggressive hunting style assuredly deserves to escape.

As an upland bird dog, the springer has few limitations. However, like any breed used to flush game, the springer must hunt within gun range to be productive. Therefore, birds of the open plains are generally not the springer's best quarry.

Comparing the springer's waterfowling capabilities with those of the Labrador, golden, or Chesapeake Bay retrievers is akin to comparing a Ford with a Ferrari. But the springer is an adequate dog for ducks and small geese under most early and mid-season conditions. With today's slim waterfowl bag limits, the springer can easily handle the modest retrieving chores of a couple of gunners in anything except near-freezing water.

When properly trained, any physically sound springer puppy backed by field-proven lineage should have both the innate temperament and necessary instincts to make it a good hunter. Nowadays, springers unfortunately are divided into two very distinct types. Those primarily from show blood should be avoided by anyone looking for a gun dog. Seek out field-bred ancestry on both the sire's and dam's side of a pedigree when you shop for a dog. Also steer clear of pups from overly large, profusely coated parents; they're bound to be strong in show breeding. The average field-type male springer won't scale more than about 45 pounds (20 kg) soaking wet. His bench-bred brethren can add another 15 pounds (7 kg) to that, and simply are not physically designed to run with the speed, agility, or stamina needed afield.

Gentle and devoted, the field-type springer strives to please his owner once he knows what's expected of him. Artful evenhandedness in training always produces the best results with this breed. The springer's somewhat sensitive nature can often bruise easily, so correction administered too forcefully insures a sulky and stubborn reaction. A frequent or continued diet of harsh treatment may well turn the springer off completely.

Competently handled with patient perseverance, the springer is an attentive, willing pupil that retains his lessons well. In fact, the springer, unlike some hunting breeds, infrequently requires training refreshers to be ready and eager to go afield each season.

Due to the springer's medium build, he can be a welcome, easily accommodated inside boarder. Although he can adjust to kennel life if acclimated early enough, fully 95 percent of the pleasure of owning a springer comes from making him part of the family. Despite an easygoing and docile nature that enables him to cope with the liveliest of youngsters, he nevertheless exhibits a personality infused with roguish good humor.

Springers generally housebreak well and make clean, well-mannered house dogs, except for the moderate shedding common to longhaired breeds (best managed by a brief daily brushing). Seldom crusty with strangers, springers nonetheless qualify as alert watchdogs, their deep-chested barks warn and give pause to all potential intruders.

Primarily white, field-bred springers usually show some black or liver ticking and patches as secondary coloring. Show dogs often sport more liver or black than white, another clue to their breeding.

The springer spaniel is sponsored in the United States by the English Springer Spaniel Field Trial Association, a member club of the American Kennel Club. Since all springers—pet, show, and hunting types—customarily are registered with the AKC, special care should be exercised to ascertain that the pup you buy for field use does indeed come from hunting lineage.

The Cocker Spaniel

Fame frequently precedes fortune for some folks. But for so many of our sporting breeds, fame too often precedes *misfortune!* The American cocker spaniel is a prime example.

As originated centuries ago in England, the cocker was simply a smaller-sized land spaniel that took his name from the sport of woodcock hunting. Randomly interbred for years, the land spaniels—springers and cockers—were a rather hodgepodge group with little real uniformity of type or size. Not until the advent of stud books and selective breeding did the situation change, with attention centering on producing dogs of specific size and type.

In 1883, the cocker was granted his own classification in English dog shows, and ten years later the breed gained the right to separate registration in the *English Kennel Club Stud Book.* Although imported to the United States by the mid-1800s, the breed never quite caught on until after the first championship field trial for cockers in 1924.

A scant decade passed before the dog show world shoved the little gun dog into the limelight. Soon everyone wanted a cocker, and the

Kissing cousins once re-moved aptly describes the American (left) and the English cocker span-iels' field capabilities to-day. Working American cockers are much scarcer than the English breed, but when found, make good field and compan-ion dogs. Photo © Kent and Donna Dannen

rush to supply the demand spawned countless "puppy mills" nation-wide. Reliable breeders still continued to breed for quality, but they proved no match for the spate of quick-buck opportunists, who largely ignored breed temperament and disposition—to say nothing of field ability—in churning out assembly-line puppies.

Further hastening the cocker's apparent ride to oblivion as a gun dog, a faction of bench-show breeders succeeded in "upgrading" the breed standard to indulge their fancy: a cocker coat of such incredible length it barely cleared the ground. Other traits of bad breeding soon manifested themselves, and excitable, bad-tempered, snappish, peren-nially piddling cockers routinely appeared. Still, the popularity train rolled on.

The clouds of war in the 1940s greatly curtailed field-trial and breed-ing activities for hunting cockers, and only the efforts of a small cadre of dedicated working cocker supporters kept cocker gun dog blood-lines intact. Their careful breeding practices and an increased promo-tion of field trials rescued hunting cockers from virtual extinction.

Simultaneously, the English cocker spaniel, a tad larger than the

American, began to appear here in increasing numbers. Having largely escaped the calamity of overpopularity, and thus preserving its natural field attributes, the English cocker provided an added shot in the arm to hunting cocker enthusiasts in the United States.

In fact, it is infinitely easier to locate breeders of working English cockers today than field dogs of the American breed. Since both are recognized as separate breeds in the United States, cocker bloodlines are also kept separate. Except for relatively minor size and conformation differences, both the American and English cocker from hunting lineage are considered basically alike, especially in their style and manner of hunting.

Once finding an American cocker of hunting ancestry, you'll discover a dog of sweet temperament and gentle disposition that is affectionate and eager to please, a seeming throwback to cockers of the 1920s and 1930s. The working American cocker is a dog for the whole family, one that can even withstand occasional ear-pulling by exuberant tots and still respond with a tongue slosh.

American cockers weigh about 26 pounds (12 kg) and stand roughly 15 inches (38 cm) at the withers. This handy size proves a blessing in restricted quarters, as well as in the car bound for the field and home again. As a hunter, the cocker searches out and flushes fur or feathers for the gun and retrieves either on land or from water. Like the springer spaniel, the cocker must work back and forth to the front and sides of the gun, never pushing beyond proper shooting range.

Generally, the medium-long coat of the typical field cocker is white with black or red markings, seen as ticking or small patches. Just like the springer, the cocker's tail is always docked.

Being a spaniel of somewhat easily bruised sensitivity, the cocker responds best to firmness dispensed gently. Rough training procedures guarantee to make him sulky and unreachable, often for hours.

Pointing Dogs

Practitioners of that classic, immobile stance that proclaims "Here's the feathered quarry," pointing dogs comb the fields and woods of the uplands, questing game birds by aerial scent. On accurate contact, the pointers "freeze," and staunchly await the gun's arrival, standing firm at the flush and shot and, when instructed, fetch the downed bird back to the hunter.

Pointing breeds cast well beyond gun-range to seek upland birds for the gunner. Here an English setter, in lofty style, points a chukar partridge. Photo © William H. Mullins

The English Setter

The big English setter loped with a deceptively long stride, halfway between the bounding of a deer and the rhythmic canter of a quarter horse. Even in the morning stillness, his padded paws fell silently on the damp leaves. Following almost as quietly were two men with shotguns, scanning the ground ahead and to both sides of the dog. They moved in unison, maintaining 20 yards (18 m) between them.

Out front, the setter began drifting to the right, then abruptly checked and, with nose climbing up into the air for that thin wisp of scent, turned away again. The dog hesitated for an instant before moving ahead cautiously—one, two, three . . . four steps. Muscles tightened with each succeeding step until, finally, locking in on the source of the scent, the setter froze just short of a stand of young hemlocks.

Even before the point, the hunters had begun maneuvering. The man on the right angled in toward the hemlocks, while his partner, picking up the pace, started in a half-circle, taking him wide of the dog and in front of the thicket. If the tactic worked, the shot would be his.

The sudden clatter of wings announced the grouse's noisy exit. But instead of flying out in front of the stand, the bird zipped back over the head of the man on the right. The gunner fired, missed, recovered in time to spin, reshoulder the shotgun, and let go the second barrel.

"Fetch, boy," he called, lowering his gun and waiting for the big setter to retrieve the prize.

For many upland hunters, the supreme moment is not the sudden, startling whir of wings, the decisive puff of feathers at the shot, or even the mix of pride and remorse that comes with holding soft, still-warm feathers in the hand. Rather, it's that moment that sets the stage for all these things: that pulse-quickening instant when a freewheeling bird dog freezes into a solid point.

Of all the breeds that adopt this classic pose on game, the English setter is possibly the best known. A favorite subject of sporting art, the setter's likeness, whether stretched out in a majestic pointing stance or serene in repose by the hearth, has probably adorned more calendars than any other gun dog. And with good reason: The English setter typifies the image of the sporting dog—good looks, strong character, noble bearing, and a depth of quiet warmth and devotion.

Certainly one of the favorite pointing dogs of the northern upland hunter, the English setter can also boast of being the oldest pointing breed in America. Many of the country's earliest settlers brought with them different strains and types of setters. These dogs, through indiscriminate mixing of bloodlines, soon came to be simply called "native" American setters. They remained hopelessly unidentifiable for years, later separating into several formidable strains that contributed to the development of today's English setter.

The breed's precise history is unknown, but several theories have evolved over the years. Perhaps the English setter resulted from a crossbreeding between the Spanish pointer, the large water spaniel, and the springer spaniel. But the more compelling theory holds that the breed was a natural outgrowth of land spaniels, a group of dogs used to flush, or spring, game into the open where, long before the advent of firearms, it could be taken by hunters' hawks.

According to the latter school, certain land spaniels that exhibited a tendency to pause or stop before rushing in to roust game were selectively bred to intensify this trait. These dogs were then used to locate game for hunters armed with nets, in lieu of hawks. Their purpose, un-

Get ready, get set for action as a gunner moves in to flush the bird in front of a staunch pointing English setter. Photo © Denver Bryan

Three English setters of the Llewellin type wait patiently in the field for their chance to hunt.
Photo © Bill Buckley/ The Green Agency

like that of the flushing spaniels, was to find and indicate the presence of "setting" game, over which the hunters then threw their nets. To distinguish these particular dogs from others, they were designated "setting spaniels."

One of the earliest written records on the subject, *Le Livre de la Chasse* (*The Book of the Hunt*), was penned about 1387 by Gaston de Foix, a French nobleman, warrior, and ardent hunting-dog fancier. His treatise not only mentions setting spaniels, but details the breed's characteristic method of handling game. By providing persuasive evidence that the setter evolved from the land spaniel, de Foix dispels all doubt that setting spaniels actually pointed game. Some two centuries later, in his volume titled *Of Englishe Dogges*, Dr. John Caius not only placed the setter in the spaniel class, but indicated that the name "setter" was actually in use at the time.

As firearms for sporting became popular in Europe, it is likely that the setter's development was greatly hastened. No longer was it necessary, or even desirable, for the dog to work as slowly and stealthily as it had for netting. In fact, hunters soon demanded faster-working setters with greater stamina and agility. By the dawn of the nineteenth century, the British Isles had produced many local and regional strains of setters. These strains eventually vanished or were absorbed into the English, Irish, and Gordon setter breeds.

Though differences exist over the origin of the breed, it is unanimously agreed that Edward Laverack was the "father of the modern English setter." Born in Keswick, England, in 1798, Laverack was spared the tedium of working as a shoemaker's apprentice when, at twenty-five, he came into a tidy legacy from a relative. Two years later he got his first English setters, Ponto and Old Moll, from the Rev. A. Harrison of Carlisle.

These two setters were reputedly the result of thirty-five years of purebreeding by the Rev. Harrison. From these two setters, Laverack produced, through an incredible process of inbreeding, a strain that became the foundation stock of the breed today, a strain which still bears his name.

In the late 1860s, a cross between Duke, Rhoebe, and several of Laverack's bitches became one of the most eminently successful setter breeding experiments. Duke and Rhoebe were setters owned respectively by Barclay Field and Thomas Statter, two prominent sportsmen of that time. This served as the inspiration and foundation for a strain ultimately named Llewellin, after R. L. Purcell Llewellin, a noted Welshman who aspired to perfect a consistent field-trial-winning strain of English setters. Obtaining two males sired by Duke out of Rhoebe, Llewellin crossed them with Laverack bitches and secured just what he had long sought. His dogs subsequently vanquished most of the competition at English field trials. Though Llewellin possessed the acumen and wherewithal to capitalize on his cross, the strain taking his name was in fact originated by Statter, Field, Armstrong, and several other contemporaries, who had utilized the Duke-Rhoebe-Laverack breeding before Llewellin was attracted to the mixture.

It is difficult to trace with accuracy the history of setter breeding before the founding of the Kennel Club in England in 1873 and the inauguration of the club's stud book the following year. The authenticity of pedigrees was often openly suspect. Many authorities believe that early breeders spiced up their stock with unrecorded infusions of whatever suited their fancies. Laverack's statement that he had inbred from his original Ponto and Old Moll for fifty-two years without resorting to a single outcross was—and still is—viewed skeptically. And, of course, it has been documented that innumerable crosses of English, Irish, Gordon, and Russian setters helped establish different strains of English setters. Rhoebe, one of the Llewellin fountainheads, for example, was half Gordon and half English setter, and this was no secret.

Still, word of Llewellin's successes soon spread across Europe and even spanned the Atlantic, precipitating an influx into America of imported dogs of the Llewellin strain. From 1877 to roughly the turn of the century, Llewellins were regarded as the crown jewels of setterdom. The strain prospered and was bred in the United States extensively. Despite the dogs' general favor, however, Llewellins and their supporters encountered fierce competition from some of the well-established "native" American setters. Especially renowned native strains were the Gildersleeves, Ethan Allens, Morfords, and Campbells, all regionally originated and named for their developers.

The battle between the proponents of Llewellins and natives reached its apex in a specially arranged field competition on December 15–16, 1879, when Gladstone—kingpin of the American Llewellins—was pitted against Joe Jr., a native mixture of Gordon, Irish, and English setter of the Campbell strain. At the end of the contest, judged solely on the number of quail each dog pointed, Joe Jr. emerged victorious, drubbing Gladstone by a nine-bird margin: sixty-one to fifty-two.

However, the Llewellin steamroller continued unabated and, in the years since, many native bloodlines have been mingled with those of Llewellins. Such inter-breeding surely has improved the English setter in America today—though it was met with disapproval in some quarters.

With so many noteworthy dogs contributing to the development of the English setter in the United States, listing them all would take much too long. But it would be inappropriate not to mention a handful of the undisputed, all-time greats. Dogs such as Gladstone, Count Noble, Ruby's Dan, Count Gladstone IV (winner of the first National Championship in America in 1896), Eugene T., Rodfield, Mohawk II, Candy Kid, Sioux, Eugene M., Eugene's Ghost, Feagin's Mohawk Pal, Phil Essig, Sports Peerless, Florendale Lou's Beau, Nugym, La Besita, Equity, and a host of others helped make the English setter what it is today.

Truly handsome, the English setter is one of the most attractive hunting breeds. His long-haired coat, which serves as protection not only

Oldest pointing breed in America, the English setter is believed to trace directly to the land spaniels in use in Europe in the early fourteenth century. Photo © John R. Falk

from the cold but from the flora in the coverts typically hunted, is predominantly white and may be flecked or patched with black, tan, orange, lemon, russet, or chestnut. The dog stands from 22 to 25 inches 56–64 cm) high at the withers and, in field condition, averages about 50 pounds (23 kg). The setter's well-balanced, symmetrical lines exemplify dash, grace, and class, and his disposition is warm, gentle, and companionable.

The breed is officially represented in the United States by the English Setter Association of America, an affiliate of the American Kennel Club. Most bench-show setters are registered with the AKC, whereas a majority of the field-bred setters are entered in the America Field's *Field Dog Stud Book.*

As a gun dog, the English setter's popularity eclipses that of all other breeds, with the exception of the English pointer—a chief rival in field trials and in the wide-open quail areas of the South. The pointer's tendency to range farther makes it ideal for unobstructed terrain, and the breed's shorthaired coat is better suited to hunting in warm southern weather. For all practical purposes, the realms of setters and pointers are divided by the Mason-Dixon line.

Partly because the National Championship field trial—the World Series of pointing-dog competitions—is held in the South, English pointers typically win top honors. But in 1970, for the first time since Mississippi Zev won the coveted title in 1946, a setter earned the laurels. That National Champion was a five-year-old, orange-and-white English setter named Johnny Crockett.

The setter's job, like that of all pointing breeds, is to seek out gamebirds by airborne scent. In fact, next to the setter's keen desire to search for birds, the instinct to point is the breed's strongest natural tendency. It is common in a kennel of field-stock English setters to witness six-to-eight-week-old pups snapping into sight-points on butterflies, grasshoppers, and other winged creatures.

In range and pace, most English setters will adjust their speed and distance to specific coverts—hunting closer and more methodically in tangled areas, ranging faster and farther in open country. Of course, a hunter can always purchase a pup whose ancestors were inclined to work at a preferred range, then accentuate these tendencies during training. In the North, this might be close-in for grouse and woodcock; in the South or Midwest it might be farther out for pheasants or quail. (Of course, a setter can learn to handle just about any gamebird that holds for a point—and even some that won't.)

Retrieving seems to come more naturally to some setters than others. Those that fetch well are, as might be expected, highly prized by their owners. With few exceptions, almost any setter can be encouraged or force-trained to retrieve downed birds, and those that won't can often be trained to "point dead" to salvage lost or crippled birds.

As for the dog's form and style, the average setter owner isn't likely to demand his dog's tail be elevated to the perfect twelve-o'clock position on every point. Only in major field trials are these most exacting elements really important. Similarly, a dog in field-trial competition must remain absolutely "steady to wing and shot," that is, remain staunchly on point throughout the flush and the shot sequence until released to resume hunting. Owners of strictly working setters, however, usually don't mind their dogs breaking point once the bird is in the air.

Setters of good field-proven ancestry normally show an early desire to hunt and, given proper training and sufficient opportunities, will usually develop nicely over time. Generally, the breed takes training and discipline in good spirits—if it is administered that way. Harsh punishment is rarely necessary or fruitful. Characterized by a soft, somewhat sensitive nature, the setter, like the spaniel, responds much better to a firm, gentle hand. And it's important to remember that setters cannot be pushed along at a pace that far exceeds their normal rate of development. Magnifying the breed's worth as a practical and highly companionable hunter is the setter's appealing charm at home.

(*The previous was adapted from the article "Out of Ponto and Old Moll," which first appeared in* Shooting Sportsman.)

The English Pointer

Say "bird dog" and pointer in the same breath almost anywhere in the rural southland, and you would be redundant. The same applies to "birds" and bobwhites. There is just no difference. Birds *are* bobwhites, and you hunt 'em with a bird dog—*a pointer.*

The natural association of the pointer and the bobwhite pretty well sums up the natural affinity each has for the other. English pointers, or as they're also known today, American pointers, are without question natural-born bird hunters. Their total being, right from conception, directs itself toward the unremitting quest for feathers. Given a choice between chow and bird hunting, most pointers would happily head for the field. Chow might run a close second—but only because it's necessary fuel for hunting.

Like the setter, whose job in the field is to find and point game birds, the pointer relies primarily on aerial body scent to locate and pinpoint targets. Because he points and holds his birds, the pointer can and often must range substantial distances from the gun. Following the flush of the birds by the gun, the well-polished pointer will remain steady until after the shot and the fetch order is given.

Precisely how long the pointer has hunted birds defies absolute answer. Many students of canine history focus on Spain in the early 1600s as the place and time of the breed's genesis. Equally unconfirmed, though strongly suspected, are the pointer's original forebears, believed to be a blend of foxhound, greyhound, and bloodhound, with a later infusion of "setting spaniels."

English pointers are natural-born bird hunters. This one displays the lofty head-and-tail-high style typical of the breed's hunting ancestry. Photo © Denver Bryan

What is certain about the pointer's definitive development is conspicuous in the breed's very name: English pointer. In England, among the hunters so instrumental in developing the English setter, were several whose parallel interest extended to refining the pointer. These included such notable gentlemen breeders as Thomas Statter, Sir Vincent Corbett, and E. Armstrong, all of whom figured prominently in the original Duke-Rhoebe-Laverack cross, ultimately popularized by R. L. Purcell Llewellin. Educated speculation strongly suggests that these and other breeders of that era surreptitiously infused some of the best setter blood into the pointer to stabilize its temperament and improve the breed's field performance.

Among the pointers coming to the United States beginning in the 1870s were several destined to establish long-lasting family bloodlines of successful field-trial and shooting dogs. Croxteth, King of Kent, Beppo III, and Mainspring formed the nucleus from which descended high-class pointers competent to compete in field trials with the cream of setterdom.

The long uphill battle for field-trial supremacy took a pivotal turn in 1909, when Manitoba Rap became the first pointer to win the National Championship. Five years later, and then again in 1916, pointers annexed the top title once more and commenced an almost uninterrupted succession of National Championships to date.

Despite the average hunter's relative indifference to field-trial records, this case in point graphically underscores the significant contributions field-trial competition can make toward improving a hunting breed. Absent the strong will to compete successfully to match the lofty standards needed to win bird dog trials, breed improvement can slow to a crawl.

Like most of our sporting breeds today, the pointer suffers the usual dichotomy of field and show breeding. But the division tends to be so clear-cut that there is little or no mixing of the two bloodlines. It is easy to locate field-bred pointers anywhere in the southern half of the country—and it is not much tougher elsewhere.

The pointer's obvious southern suitability owes to its shorthaired coat and its propensity for working well in warmer climes. Virtually burr-resistant, the breed's short coat proves quick and easy to groom. Less protection against cold northern weather and heavy cover punishment inflicted in typical grouse and woodcock areas are the coat's marginal downsides.

The pointer's most significant hunting assets are speed, range, and early development, along with strong natural pointing instinct. Favorably weighting the entire equation is the pointer's ability to endure the push-along type of schooling incurred by the less-patient owner. Seldom thin-skinned, pointers take correction in stride and generally shrug off a grudge.

White—the preferred color for visibility afield—predominates the pointer's shorthaired coat, with patches and/or tickings of solid liver, orange, lemon, or black overlays. Neat streamlining belies the breed's well-muscled body structure, complemented by a classic, tapered, full-length tail. Standing from 24 to 26 inches (61–66 cm) at the withers, pointer dogs tip the scales at an average of about 60 pounds (27 kg). Bitches trim 5 to 7 pounds (2–3 kg) and an inch (2.5 cm) or so off those figures.

Though characterized by a friendly disposition, pointers tend toward boldness and independence in everything they do. While affectionate to a degree with owners and family, kissy dogs they are not. Pointers make excellent kennel dogs, but can also live indoors, if their highly active ways are acceptable.

The American Pointer Club, a member club of the American Kennel Club, officially sponsors the breed in the United States. Field-bred pointers are almost exclusively registered with the American Field's *Field Dog Stud Book*.

The Brittany

Not too many years ago, a profile on the Brittany spaniel might have begun by describing the breed as "the only pointing member of the spaniel family." A while back, though, the powers that can dictate such things decreed that spaniel, the Brittany's last name, be officially dropped. Now, like such mod entertainment luminaries as Madonna and Cher, the breed goes by just a one-name moniker: Brittany.

Although they may have taken the spaniel out of the name, they can't take it out of the Brittany's heritage. Smallest of the pointing breeds, the Brittany differs from the spaniel clan's conventional hunting style of charging right in and pushing birds into flight. But in temperament, the Brittany is all spaniel: intelligent, alert, animated, affectionate, and eager to please.

Muddled in the usual morass of legend, conjecture, and historical confusion, the Brittany's origin theoretically traces to the time of the Irish invasion of Gaul in the fifth century A.D. Various seventeenth-century tapestries and other pieces of artwork depict dogs of definite Brittany type. These representations are numerous enough to suggest that Brittanies were far from uncommon in parts of Europe at that time.

Around 1850, in the small Brittany town of Pontou, an abnormality produced the breed's first two tailless pups. The one that survived to maturity gained prominence, both for his field abilities and his prowess at producing tailless and stubtailed progeny. This became one of the Brittany's lasting unique physical aspects.

Some fifty years later, a Frenchman named Arthur Enaud launched an improvement program to combat the deterioration resulting from excessive inbreeding of Brittanies. Unfortunately, lack of good record-keeping obscured the several outcrosses he employed in reinvigorating

Fully competent to work afield on any North American game bird, the Brittany is an able retriever. His compact build also makes him an ideal size for a housepet. Photo © Denver Bryan

Brittany attributes. His success is reflected today in the breed's keen scenting ability and strong pointing instinct.

The first-known pair of Brits imported into the United States arrived in 1912, but most of the earlier Brits began arriving in modest numbers around 1930. Two decades passed before the public began to take note of the breed, largely through the efforts of two New Jersey hunters/breeders who formed the Brittany Spaniel Club of North America.

In 1942, that group merged with the newly formed American Brittany Club and developed a new breed standard, which was officially adopted four years later. A gradual gain in popularity followed, though the Brit's reputation for very deliberate pace and restricted range dampened its appeal.

Striving to bring the Brittany up to a competitive level with the faster, wider-ranging pointing breeds participating in field trials initially provided the Brit a needed shot in the arm. Today, however, some critics contend that the pendulum has swung too far and that a majority of Brits have been bred more to field-trial standards than to those of the average hunter. Certainly that may be true in some strains, but a careful shopper should face little difficulty finding a Brittany of suitable range and pace.

Fully competent to work on any North American game bird, the Brittany exhibits an animated, all-business style of hunting, accenting a sense of determination to do his job well. An able, natural retriever, the Brit can be force-trained to fetch if deemed necessary. But force training should be done slowly, with emphasis on the *training*, rather than on the *force*. The Brittany's spaniel nature does not take well to strong-arming.

The breed's longhaired coat, basically white with either liver or orange markings, provides adequate protection from cold weather and heavy brush. And his compact build—an average 35 pounds (16 kg) and 17½ to 20½ inches (44–52 cm) at the withers—translates to "ideal housepet size." The Brittany fills the role well: adaptable and devoted to all family members.

Since the breed's popularity has risen steadily, it is important to verify the field-proven ancestry of a Brittany before buying the dog for hunting. While most Brittanies are registered with the American Kennel Club, many hunting Brits are listed with the American Field's *Field Dog Stud Book*.

The German Shorthaired Pointer

As the draft horse is to the heaviest workload, the German shorthaired pointer is to the strictly results-oriented upland bird hunter. A no-nonsense, real meat-and-potatoes gun dog, the shorthair is as steady and reliable a producer of game as can be found anywhere.

True to his Teutonic roots, the German shorthair is a paragon of stability and determination, as diligent and deliberate as he is thorough in his work afield. Like all pointing breeds, the shorthair covers his ground in a quartering pattern, seeking fresh scent and indicating the nearby presence of birds by establishing a solid pointing stance. Then, after the successful shot and the gunner's order, he retrieves the feathered prize promptly and softly to hand.

While most other pointing breeds hunt high-headed to quaff body scent carried on the breeze, the shorthair concentrates on foot scent to trail and locate birds. This head-down hunting technique detracts somewhat from the breed's overall style in comparison to the more classic

Diligent, deliberate, and thorough in his work afield, the German shorthaired pointer has become a virtual fixture on commercial hunting preserves. Photo © Denver Bryan

setters and pointers. But if results form the bottom line, who can argue?

As the shorthair's name indicates, Germany was the breed's birthplace about 300 years ago. General concurrence credits the Spanish pointer as the main foundation stock of the breed. Speculation takes over from there, with the probable introduction of hound blood, either the old St. Hubert hound or the bloodhound, or possibly both, along with others of local origin.

Dependable facts about the breed's development became available only after the development of the *Klub Kurzhaar Stud Book* in the 1870s. At least one outcross was made with the English pointer to further refine the shorthair, giving the breed more agility and somewhat less reliance on ground trailing. Further selective breeding provided additionally desired qualities and stabilized breed uniformity.

The early shorthair imports to the United States in the 1920s created scant interest. Lacking suitable range and pace for American hunting conditions and tastes, the breed languished until its utilitarian traits were largely bartered in favor of bird hunting specialization.

Today's Americanized shorthair has notched a permanent place in the affections of North American upland bird hunters. A virtual fixture on commercial hunting preserves, the shorthair can stand up dependably to long hours of work in all kinds of cover.

A big dog, standing as tall as 26 inches (66 cm) at the withers and scaling as much as 70 pounds (32 kg), the shorthair has a placid disposition and is somewhat stoic in temperament. A definite attribute, the breed's adaptability allows him to overcome even the most inept schooling and still graduate as a practical gun dog.

White with patches and tickings of liver, his shorthaired coat grooms easily right down to his always-docked tail. Despite the shorthair's large size, he makes a fine family pet and alert watchdog. He tolerates kennel life right from puppyhood, but, once having sampled indoor living with family, most shorthairs rebel at subsequent exclusion.

The breed is officially sponsored in the United States by the German Shorthaired Pointer Club of America, a member club of the American Kennel Club. Beside registration in the AKC, shorthairs can be registered with the American Field's *Field Dog Stud Book*.

As with most sporting breeds, substantial numbers of shorthairs are bred primarily from show stock, making it important to look for field-proven ancestry when purchasing one for hunting.

The vizsla, whose origins date back to the tenth century, combines nose, intelligence, and strong hunting desire with natural pointing and retrieving instincts. Photo © Dale C. Spartas/The Green Agency

The Vizsla

A dock-tailed English pointer, moistened slightly, then dipped and thoroughly rolled in cinnamon might serve as a chef's description of the vizsla, the official pointing dog of Hungary and now a respected, naturalized U.S. citizen.

The recipe for this handsome pointing breed? Nose and intelligence, plus strong, natural pointing and retrieving instincts well blended with spirited hunting desire, all neatly folded into a sleek, rusty-gold or cinnamon-colored shorthaired coat.

In the field, the vizsla adheres to the typical job description of pointing breeds: namely, to seek out game birds by scent and staunchly point their location for the gun, then, on command after the flush, to make a gentle retrieve of the downed bird.

Reportedly one of the oldest sporting breeds, the vizsla dates back some ten centuries to its origin among the Magyar tribes that invaded and settled the vast plains of Hungary. Stone etchings of the period picture a Magyar hunter with a falcon and vizsla-type dog, and manuscripts from the 1300s describe dogs strongly resembling the vizsla.

51

For centuries, stewardship of the breed was the responsibility of the Magyars, but this later fell to the Hungarian aristocracy. The year 1825 marked the establishment of the *Magyar Vizsla Stud Book* and the beginning of the breed's modern history. Endangered almost to the point of extinction by World Wars I and II and the 1944–45 Soviet invasion of Hungary, the vizsla survived only by escaping in small numbers with their refugee owners and fleeing to other European nations.

Some ten years after arriving in the United States in 1950, the vizsla was accepted for registration in the American Kennel Club. Support developed quickly for the vizsla among upland bird hunters, since the breed arrived as a bird-hunting specialist and wasn't forced to shed the mantle of jack-of-all-trades like the earlier continentals.

Well-adapted to close-cover hunting by virtue of his deliberate pace and relatively restricted range, the vizsla nicely fits the requirements of many of today's gunners. The breed will seldom bypass tight-sitting birds, nor do many wounded birds escape his ultra-sharp nose. If graceful style suffers in comparison to that of setter or pointer, determination and naturally strong scenting prowess, combined with superior retrieving proclivities, surely balance the vizsla's scales of productivity.

The vizsla is comparable to most medium-sized pointing breeds, weighing an average 55 pounds (25 kg) and standing from 22 to 24 inches (56–61 cm) at the withers. His tail, generally docked to 6 or 8 inches (15–20 cm), becomes abuzz when the dog zeroes in on game.

Adept at absorbing lessons taught with kindliness, the vizsla wilts under heavy-handedness. And although inclined a bit toward stubbornness, the breed's sensitive nature requires patient firmness worn under a velvet glove. Effusively affectionate, the vizsla makes an excellent, if lively, home companion, ever alert and protective of his family.

Officially sponsored in the United States by the Vizsla Club of America, the breed is accepted for registration in both the American Kennel Club and the American Field's *Field Dog Stud Book*. The standard advice to avoid excessive show breeding and to concentrate on field-proven hunting lineage applies when buying the vizsla as a gun dog.

The Wirehaired Pointing Griffon
Remember "Daisy," the Bumpsted's lovable shaggy dog from the movie version of the Blondie comic strip? If so, then you already have a rea-

A hard, wiry outer coat overlaying a short undercoat allows the wirehaired pointing griffon to handle all types of cover and weather. Here a griff racks up a nice point in a snow-dotted field. Photo © Bill Marchel

sonable mental image of the wirehaired pointing griffon. Identical twins? No, but close enough.

In spite of the griff's atypical bird dog appearance, don't be misled. This shaggy fellow is not only a bird dog but a versatile one at that! Imbued with strong retrieving instinct and an inherent fondness of swimming, the griff excels at fetching ducks in all but the worst imaginable weather and water conditions.

Aided by a retriever-type short undercoat topped by a hard, wiry outer coat, the griff can scoff at the most punishing of heavy cover in the uplands. Quartering the ground before the gun, he utilizes both foot and body scent to find and point birds. And his always-deliberate, close-working style qualifies the griff as an appropriate choice for much of today's constricted hunting covers.

E. K. Korthals, a Dutch emigre to Germany, is considered the unchallenged originator of the breed. Tarred with his father's avocational interest in animal husbandry, Korthals began his development work with specimens of the rough-coated griffon, a breed believed to stem from the ancient griffon hounds. Slipshod record-keeping unfortunately clouded much of the information about the various outcrosses Korthals used. Tidbits pieced together, however, conclude that Korthals employed setter, spaniel, otterhound, and, possibly, an infusion of German short-haired pointer in his breeding program.

The very first wirehaired pointing griffon to reach U.S. shores arrived in 1887 and was registered that year by the American Kennel Club under the name Zolette. It was only after the turn of the century, though, that appreciable numbers of the breed appeared here. Still, it took the establishment of the Wirehaired Pointing Griffon Club of America, soon after World War II, to achieve any significant support for the breed.

What the griff lacks in luster is more than compensated by disposition and personality. Willingness could well be the griff's middle name, for no matter what's asked of him, he tries to oblige, generally with success. Perhaps the dog's intelligence, which seems to grow with time and maturity, owes in part to the close relationship he forms with owner and family.

Indoors, with his people, is really where the breed thrives and belongs, if space can possibly permit. His size notwithstanding—a height from 21 to 23 inches (53–58 cm) at the withers and weighing an average 55 pounds (25 kg)—the griff usually exhibits a calm demeanor, compatible even in the closest of quarters. The griffon's bristly, medium-length coat is essentially steel gray or muted white with splotches of chestnut, and his tail is always docked to about 6 or 8 inches (15–20 cm).

American Kennel Club registration is the norm for most griffs, but the breed also is accepted for registry in the American Field's *Field Dog Stud Book*. The safest course for potential buyers is through the Wirehaired Pointing Griffon Club of America, which can supply a list of approved breeders of field-proven griffons.

3

Choosing the Right Veterinarian

Proper lifelong maintenance of your gun dog's health requires the services of a competent veterinarian. Sounds easy enough when you say it fast. There are lots of vets and animal hospitals around, right? Sure. Medical doctors and hospitals also abound, but you're probably pretty particular about which ones you visit for the health care of your family and yourself. The same care should be taken in choosing the right vet.

One of the most important aspects of the veterinarian selection process is doing it early, preferably even before acquiring your soon-to-be hunting partner. Though that bright, soulful-eyed little guy or gal will probably have already had some immunization shots, your gun dog's shot series will have to be completed soon after you acquire him or her. You'll also want an immediate "insurance" once-over to confirm the pup's good health.

The first step is to locate a good veterinarian. Take note, I said a *good* vet, not necessarily the *right* vet. Only time will tell whether the initial, good vet is the right one for you. Meanwhile, you'll need a reasonable starting point, and you can always switch later if the good vet turns out not to be quite right.

Dog-owning neighbors, friends, and nearby relatives can often recommend the vet they use. They can also let you know of which vet or vets to steer clear in your search. That sometimes is even more valuable information than a wishy-washy endorsement. One thing to keep in mind in either case, though, is that sometimes veterinarians get bad recommendations from clients who neglected to have their dogs treated for serious ailments or who failed to follow instructions or continue treatment. This is why it's imperative that you know and accurately gauge the source of your advice.

Besides word-of-mouth to locate a vet, there's the good old Yellow

Left: *The taxidermy and general hunting motif of this veterinary facility should bode well for the gun dog owner and his golden retriever. Having a vet who hunts and understands gun dogs can be a definite plus.* Photo © Bill Buckley/ The Green Agency

Right: *Every new gun dog, whether puppy or adult, should receive an early examination by a veterinarian, along with whatever inoculations prove appropriate. This budding young hunter ably assists his Lab's vet in the process.* Photo © Mitch Kezar

Pages. They are not, of course, endorsements, but merely listings of the veterinary practices in the local area. Other possibilities include area dog breeders, kennel owners, obedience school instructors, and pet shop operators. All of them need good, reliable veterinary services. The American Animal Hospital Association (AAHA) is another helpful resource. It can provide you with the name of the nearest AAHA member vet in your area. The AAHA address and phone number are listed in the appendix. Your telephone information service and/or the local library will have the phone number and address of your state veterinary medical association, which can also provide names of veterinary practitioners in your area.

After collecting a list of potential veterinarians, start sorting out the two, three, or four most likely candidates. In a suburb of a large metropolitan area, you may even have more options. Rural areas may severely limit your choices. In any event, proximity to your home may narrow your alternatives and prove to be the deciding factor in your selection. Convenience is important to many, but such handiness is of the greatest significance when you need emergency medical help for your dog. This also brings up another pertinent aspect of choosing a vet: Does your chosen vet offer after-hours emergency treatment? If not, how far away is an emergency veterinary clinic? Would the clinic have quick access to your dog's medical records? Or, must they wait, sometimes critically, to get information from your vet during regular office hours? These are vital questions that you must address before selecting the vet to whom you trust your gun dog's health.

Before your final decision, you should also request a tour of the veterinary facilities. The entire operation should be well-organized and the sanitation as scrupulous as reasonably possible. The office doesn't have to reek of disinfectant, but the clinic should be free of offensive odors and have an overall aura of cleanliness.

The degree of trust a good vet inspires in you will weigh heavily in how comfortable you feel with him or her. After your initial choice, your evaluation will come to rest on such factors as "bedside manner." Yes, even vets (good ones, anyway) possess that quality. How they view your dog, whether sincerely—with genuine understanding and compassion— or clinically, can turn you on or off. Many experienced dog owners say they prefer female veterinarians, since they believe women generally ex- hibit a soft, gentle technique in dealing with animals. Today, there are approximately 11,000 women in the veterinary profession as private clinic practitioners, comprising a little more than 25 percent of all li- censed veterinarians in private practice.

Additional services available—besides the all-important medical ones—may also become a factor. These might include regular boarding facilities and/or the services of a professional groomer on the premises. As might be imagined, a boarding kennel run by your own veterinarian could spare you the rigors of finding a suitable facility for weekend or vacation boarding. The assumption is that the boarding operation meets the same high standards of quality you receive for your dog's health care.

Naturally, the fees your vet charges must be among your overall considerations. Most vets will provide you with a printed list of various

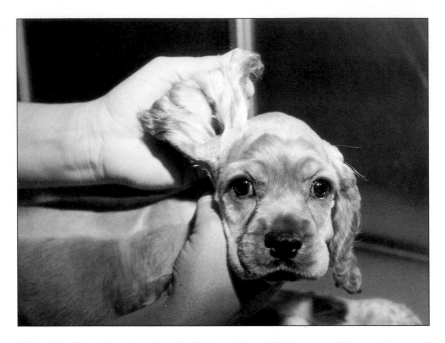

The trust a good vet inspires both in owner and dog goes a long way toward establishing a confident relationship for your dog's lifelong health care. Photo © Norvia Behling

procedures and prices upon request. If such a list is not available, it's up to you to ask about the charges for routine items, such as office visits for check ups and inoculations. Certainly, a realistic estimate of any unusual, serious, or complicated procedure should be given in advance of treatment.

Part of the confidence your chosen vet will eventually instill in you will owe to the vet's ability to communicate—with you. Instructions about treatment and medication you may be required to administer at home should be clearly and patiently conveyed. The vet should always be willing to discuss any of your dog's health problems in nontechnical language, making certain you fully understand any diagnosis and recommended treatment.

Hopefully, the time and effort you initially spend in finding a *good* veterinarian will pay dividends in confirming that you did, indeed, pick the *right* one. But if not, for your dog's sake and your own stress level, begin the search anew.

4

The How, When, Where, and Which of Pup Picking

The young of all mammalian species are, perhaps arguably, cute. But for sheerly irresistible cute-power, puppies, whatever the breed, top the list. Even the most macho of men become pure putty under the inexorable spell of a puppy. In addition, a puppy's marvelous blend of trust and wide-eyed innocence plays unmercifully on some women's maternal instincts. But as timeless as puppies' appeal may be, there is a choice time for a hunter to buy a four-footed future gunning partner.

That initial autumn chill that augers promise of a soon-to-begin bird season typically jump-starts the prospective puppy buyer's search engine. His imagination, whirling away, envisions a bouncy, lovable puppy, the sort to instantly win over the family and to take hunting by midseason.

But, unfortunately, an eight-week-old pup purchased in September could hardly be expected to hunt that same season. Except for older or "started" dogs at least seven to ten months of age, September is just too late to buy a puppy for the fall season.

The breeding schedules for a majority of professionals, as well as many knowledgeable, amateur gun dog breeders aims to have pups ready months earlier. Since spring's warm temperatures provide more-favorable rearing conditions for puppies, the breeders schedule their bitches to whelp early enough to have pups weaned and ready to go to new homes between mid-April and early July. Though Mother Nature's plan is noncommercial, her own wildlife production timetable is very similar.

Breeders strive to move out their pups as soon after weaning as possible, generally at about six to eight weeks. Beyond that point, costs be-

A passel of comfortably snoozing golden retriever pups epitomizes that irresistible force called "cute power." Photo © Henry H. Holdsworth

gin to rise briskly, contributing to a full-scale buyer's market, the best time for you to buy that gun dog puppy.

The early days of summer provide other advantages for buying a new puppy. The added daylight hours offer more time to spend outdoors with the pup, to reinforce a housebreaking routine, to familiarize him with collar and lead, and also to condition him to brief rides in the car.

Moreover, acclimating the pup to his new surroundings will be much easier if you can arrange your purchase for a time when you'll be at home for a prolonged period. At all costs, avoid buying the pup just before leaving home on vacation if you'll have to put him in a boarding kennel while you're gone. A puppy undergoing the shock of separation from Mom and littermates needs to imprint early with his new family. Another separation, with the added stress of lonely days in a boarding kennel, could irreversibly damage the puppy's development.

MALE OR FEMALE?

After deciding on an appropriate breed, you will have to address the question of dog or bitch. Nine times out of ten, especially for the first-time buyer, a dog is virtually an automatic choice. It is assumed to be not just the best, but the *only* choice—and male chauvinism has nothing to do with it. Why a male? Unfortunately, it is purely unfamiliarity with the canine "fairer sex." Many know little about female dogs, except that bitches have menstrual cycles and can get pregnant—usually with unwelcome outside assistance. Yet, this well-conditioned mental reflex just may deprive you of the kind of hunting companion you really had in mind. The decision of male or female should never be made without an objective comparison of each sex's distinctive characteristics. Realizing that most potential owners feel they can relate more closely to the male persona, principally because most potential owners are male themselves, let's transpose things and take a closer look at how the bitch stacks up.

Biologically, a female undergoes two twenty-one-day heat periods each year. Approximately six months apart, the female's estrus cycles are intended by nature for procreation. A bitch will, therefore, attempt to mate during these periods, unless she's securely confined. Yet, it's not generally much of a problem to limit her to one area, such as the kitchen, where her spotting can easily be cleaned, or to a secure, covered, backyard kennel run. Admittedly, the heat periods are an inconvenient minor annoyance to some owners, and to others, a profound drawback. For the latter, spaying the bitch is always an option. But it's an irreversible operation, which means no matter how much you might someday want her to produce a litter of pups, she can't oblige.

Most bitches are smaller framed and weigh from 5 to 10 pounds (2–5 kg) less than males of their breed. Often these dimensions can prove an advantage, should limited space necessitate a more compactly built dog to live indoors. Similarly, the handier-sized female is somewhat easier and more convenient to transport. The smaller car crate she requires leaves more spare room for guns, hunting gear, and other essentials.

Ordinarily more inclined toward cleanliness than dogs, bitches usually housebreak easily and quickly. Generally, they also tend to "oblige" quicker with the task at hand during their daily walks, an estimable advantage in nasty weather.

Bitches also differ in temperament from dogs. Invariably more tractable, females are more likely to shower affection on their folks with greater abandon than their male counterparts. And bitches unquestionably display more dependency on their owners, their submissive natures expanding an already heightened eagerness to please. They're less able than males to take brusque correction or overly stern punishment. With the advantage of maturing sooner than dogs, and consequently allowing a possible earlier start to their schooling, bitches often seem quicker and a bit easier to train. It is generally acknowledged that they grasp their lessons a touch faster. Still, they also appear to reach a learning climax, or cutoff point, more quickly than dogs. While the male id perpetually drives him to prowl, the female is predisposed—with those semiannual exceptions—to linger close to home and family.

Now, chivalry appeased by scrutinizing the ladies first, let's appraise the males.

The fact that dogs don't get pregnant doubtless constitutes the single, most overwhelming advantage favoring male selection. But, although bitches menstruate twice a year, their most ardent disciples quickly point out that dogs are always "in heat." However, dogs will strategically ignore the onerous aspects of an unforeseen pregnancy. The obligations of fatherhood are virtually unknown in the dog world, and rare, indeed, are canine paternity suits.

Dogs are larger-boned, heavier, and more muscular than bitches.

Most professional breeders like to move their pups out to new homes as soon after weaning as possible. This trio of seven-week-old golden retriever puppies gets a once-over from prospective owners. Photo © Lon E. Lauber

They also tend to have bolder temperaments and moderately greater physical endurance. Often enough, the housebreaking task is found to be more difficult with dogs. The male's natural instinct to mark his territory by frequent leg-lifts often extends to portions of his owner's domain. While seldom delighting his boss, such behavior usually charms milady even less.

Boasting more rugged natures, dogs can ordinally tolerate stricter discipline and less-gentle training procedures. Although their learning pace may lag a bit behind bitches', dogs' intensity levels in later years can bypass that of their female counterparts.

Distinctly more independent by nature, dogs typically reveal a greater degree of self-assertiveness in the field. Depending less on their handlers, dogs tend to hunt more aggressively with a minimum of direction. Ergo, while bitches are often more easily trained, the greater independence males display in the field may provide counterbalance.

Finally, while males are more prone to scrap with others of their sex, bitches generally seem to regard peace and harmony as a better alternative.

Above: *A pretty sight point foretells a strong natural pointing instinct in this German shorthair pup.* Photo © William H. Mullins
Right: *Checking a pup's reactions when apart from littermates is an important part of the purchase selection process. This sassy golden pup seems to say, "Okay, what's next?"* Photo © Henry H. Holdsworth

So, it's your choice. Although choosing a gun dog's sex is probably not as self-evident a matter as you originally perceived, at least now your decision can be a considered one, designed to help start you off with the kind of hunting companion you've always dreamed of having.

WHERE TO FIND THAT PUP

The first step in finding a suitable gun dog pup of the breed you want is to locate a reputable breeder. At all costs, avoid any thought of going to one of those pet franchises or big department stores. The help in those establishments don't have a clue about gun dogs, and it's virtually guaranteed that their stock will be strictly from pet or show bloodlines.

You'd also be wise to skip what are called "backyard breeders," locals—whose bitches may have had an unexpected pregnancy, or a litter

born of indiscriminate breeding—who sell to make some fast-buck profits. That's not to say that all such folks should be so branded; many amateurs who breed gun dogs knowledgeably produce good hunting puppies. But, without consulting references personally familiar with the field abilities of the litter's parents, you'd probably do better to search elsewhere.

Where should you start? Probably the best route is to contact the secretary of the club that sponsors the breed of your choice. A letter briefly describing your wants and requesting reliable sources to investigate should bring you a list of breeders and/or kennels in your locality. Of course, it's helpful and considerate to include a self-addressed, stamped envelope with your request. Information on breed club secretaries can be obtained from the American Kennel Club, the American Field Publishing Co., and the United Kennel Club, a listing of which appears in the appendix.

If, perchance, you strike out with the club secretary—a rare occurence—you might try a number of other avenues: for example, local sporting goods retailers; the outdoor editors of area newspapers; gun club and hunting preserve operators; and the advertisements in specialty breed journals.

It is good practice to write or telephone the recommended sources to narrow the list to two or three who can best accomodate your requirements. A brief phone conversation with a breeder can save you a wasted personal visit, should all his puppies already be sold, or not exactly fulfill your desires.

Once you settle on one particular breeder or kennel, you can schedule an appointment to visit and select your pup. When you go, don't clutch over the idea of having to choose the "best" puppy in a litter. Some people, in recent years, have tried to reduce puppy picking to an exact science, devising multifaceted tests purported to "read" a puppy's future personality. If your own personality reflects a highly structured, technical approach to decision making, go right ahead and try the method; it can't hurt. (Your local library can probably help you find written details of the procedure.) However, most experienced dog people still subscribe to the belief that puppy picking is an inexact science, at best. There are no guarantees involved, not even for the veteran professional, just a few traditional suggestions.

The best first step in puppy selection is to look at the litter's parents.

Though the sire may not always be on the premises, it is unusual for the dam not to be there. Her overall conformation, coloring, and demeanor are solid clues to her pups' makeup. Take time to study and interact with her before even looking at the litter.

When you check out the puppies, focus only on those of the preferred sex that most closely mirror in size, general appearance, and coloring, one or both parents and the rest of the litter. Rule out the smallest and the biggest pups, and concentrate on those most alike. The uniformity of those puppies usually ensures that they will grow to be typical of their breed and close clones of their sire and dam.

Then play with the pups. Watch carefully for signs of shyness, nervousness, or unfriendliness. With these rules of thumb in mind, choose the two puppies you like best. Leave briefly and find a vantage point where, unseen, you can observe how those two pups interact with one another and their littermates. If they're both still in contention after your observations—in other words you detect no obvious faults—request to see each one separately, out in the yard away from their brothers and sisters.

What you want to see in a pup is a natural curiosity, plus a bold or, at least, not overly timid reaction to strange surroundings and unfamiliar objects. Study and play with each of the two pups for a few minutes. Now, it's showtime: You must pick the one you want. If you still cannot decide, the puppies are probably so similar that either would make an excellent choice. After choosing, you and the breeder should examine the pup thoroughly for any possible physical defects that escaped notice earlier.

In winding things up, be sure the breeder provides you with all the pertinent information about the pup. Get in writing the types, brand names, and dates of all the shots and wormings your puppy has received. Be certain you know your pup's specific diet and, perhaps, request a small sample to tide the pup over until you get to the store. Also, ask for the signed certificates you will need to complete your pup's registration in the appropriate stud book.

For the pup's ride home, a newspaper-lined corrugated box will usually suffice. But an accompanying spouse's lap—appropriately protected—serves infinitely more lovingly.

5

The Significance of a Name

For some owners, naming their pup is marked by indifference. A call name—the one used every day, literally, to call the dog—seems an issue of minor concern. Names like Rover, Queenie, or Pal are deemed adequate, though they show little imagination. Equivalently, a dull registration name reflects little or nothing about the anticipated potential of a pup when it matures, or, for that matter, offers few clues about its ancestry. I suspect that the majority of new owners probably need only a gentle nudge to devote a bit more deliberation to the naming and registration process. Hopefully, I can provide some assistance here.

THE OFFICIAL NAME

The official, registered name you choose for your pup will customarily be limited to three or four words, with a specified maximum of letters and/or numbers, according to each registry. Suppose your pup's ancestry was a renowned line of grouse dogs tracing to a prepotent stud, say Bonasa, for instance. Logically, including Bonasa, or some variant of it, in your pup's official name would make sense. Sometimes, a prominent kennel name can be added, too, although that option may require written permission from the kennel owner.

Working a dog's call name into his official name is the favored approach of some owners. Exercising the imagination can add a touch of originality, as well as enhance the personal satisfaction of coming up with a catchy handle. A name befitting a Labrador retriever, for example, could be "Markwell Aqua Bat," Markwell being the kennel name, and

A name befitting a Labrador retriever may well be "Markwell Aqua Bat," Markwell being the kennel name and "Bat," the pup's actual call name. Photo © Denver Bryan

By authenticating the accuracy of your dog's lineage, you increase the dog's value. This is a documented purebred German shorthaired pointer. Photo © Denver Bryan

Bat being the pup's actual call name. How about "Duckcrest's Amber Joy" for a yellow Lab bitch of Duckcrest ancestry? Maybe "Briar Ridge Buster" or "Up 'N Adam" for a soon-to-be pheasant hunting springer spaniel. Only lack of creativity can limit the possibilities.

Yet, whether or not your pup's call name is part of his registration name, it should be short, snappy, and commanding in tone, but not a command sound-alike. It should also be quick and easy to say—or bellow.

REGISTRATION

Why register your dog? Is there any real purpose to it? Yes, indeed! Registering your dog establishes a permanent record identifying him with an official name and number that certifies his ancestry (pedigree). By authenticating the accuracy of your dog's lineage, you increase your dog's value. In addition, registration makes any field-trial placements he may win part of the official record. Lastly, should he ever sire any puppies, registration makes selling them easier, faster, and more profitable, since, at least in some stud books, if a sire isn't registered, his puppies cannot be registered, either.

To complete your dog's registration, you will need certain certificates; requirements vary by registry organizations. As mentioned earlier, be sure to get the proper forms from the breeder or kennel owner before taking your pup home.

Most hunting breeds are registered in one of the three major registration organizations. It is traditional to register your puppy in the same registry as his sire and dam. Actually, because the trail of red tape is deeper than a well-digger's well, it's hardly worth the difficulty to try to register a puppy in a different organization's registry. The three major registries are the American Kennel Club, which registers all purebreds it currently recognizes; *The Field Dog Stud Book* of the American Field Publishing Company, which accepts all purebreds for registration, but specializes in the pointing breeds; and the United Kennel Club, which registers all breeds, but specializes in hounds and working retrievers.

Registering your new pup immediately after purchase certainly isn't necessary, but, don't delay too long, or you just may never get to it.

No excuse can justify creating a grossly overweight house dog. This golden retriever does, however, have a built-in excuse: she's pregnant and probably contemplating the responsibilities of motherhood. Photo © Henry H. Holdsworth

6

Your Gun Dog as Live-In Companion

The idea that keeping a gun dog in the house is a serious no-no stems more from tradition than from fact. Unfortunately, it's a common notion that keeps the owner and the dog from achieving the close relationship that can be realized by sharing living quarters year-round. Exiling a gun dog to a doghouse or backyard kennel is too often standard practice for many owners. If it is at all possible, share your home and hearth with the gun dog; it constitutes an opportunity no owner should pass up.

Assuredly, the arrangement is not necessarily problem-free. Examples of the fate of the average house dog are all too prevalent. Just take a gander at some of them: immoderately pudgy, largely untrained, grossly undisciplined, and either pampered or woefully neglected. Couldn't the same fate plague a gun dog kept in the house? Perhaps. But let's take a moment to examine how so many of those hapless canines wind up that way, and why the prudent owner's hunting dog need not.

No rational excuse can justify creating a flagrantly overweight house dog. Excluding disease or hormonal imbalance, dogs gain weight for the same reasons we humans do: overeating and underexercising.

No question about it, overfeeding a house dog owes principally to its close presence. But applying some basic willpower to avoid impulsively giving treats can overcome the problem—and the whole family should refrain from handing out snacks. Banning tidbits and holding special goodies to a minimum goes along with feeding your dog a sensible diet. The diet should be adapted to the type and frequency of the gun dog's daily exercise and field work. Hunting a dog hard during the season, then cutting him down to a thrice daily walk to his favored potty spot during the rest of the year, without altering the type and quantity of his food, just won't work—nor will simply reducing his ration during the offseason. Only a combination of proper diet and regular exercise will keep a dog in good muscle tone and trim physical shape year-round.

Ill-mannered behavior, so often seen in house pets, recalls the old axiom, "Familiarity breeds contempt," a favorite of the "gun-dogs-should-never-be-kept-indoors" crowd. The rationale cited asserts that a dog's respect for obedience dips substantially with too close a relationship to his owner. Of course, that strikes most thinking folks as curious, since rapport normally evolves from close association. However, an indifferent attitude toward enforcing obedience will weaken discipline. If the owner seems unconcerned about compliance every time a command is given, it's a sure bet the dog won't be too concerned with obedience. Year-round, indoor living should hardly excuse relaxing normal control. Whenever an order is given, the dog should obey it immediately. Condoning less-than-proper compliance in the home will surely reflect in the dog's behavior in the field.

Still another absurdity declares that dogs quartered in the home suffer diminishing scenting ability plus decreasing instinct and desire to hunt. The likelihood of a dog's nose seriously deteriorating indoors is as logical as the opposite theory that living outdoors will improve it. Unless affected by a debilitating illness or injury, a dog's olfactory potential remains immutable throughout his lifetime, regardless of where the majority of that lifetime is spent. Sometimes it may seem that, like old cheese, a dog's nose improves with age. When that seems to happen, experience is really what made that nose more efficient.

But what about the assertion that house dogs inevitably sustain diminished instinct and desire to hunt? In the majority of field-bred gun dogs, a heritage developed over hundreds of years fuels the innate instinct to eagerly hunt. Thus, it strains credibility to suggest that such venerable natural instincts could be perceptibly weakened within the brief span of one dog's lifetime lived indoors.

No, the claim that sharing the home ensures a gun dog's eventual ruination simply doesn't hold water—if his owner properly handles his responsibilities. In fact, shared indoor living offers some very practical advantages, such as observing and identifying certain of your gun dog's little quirks and reactive behavior patterns. These things could easily escape notice if the dog is relegated to a kennel. And it's often these small but meaningful insights into a hunting dog's true personality that

With proper care and discipline, sharing the old homestead makes for better rapport between gun dog and owner. These two youngsters seem quite content with their living arrangements and each other. Photo © William H. Mullins

help shorten or modify training techniques for quicker or more dependable results.

Indisputably, the intimate relationship that house dog and owner develop can form a deeper understanding between them. Although discipline should never be sacrificed, the bond will grow stronger, and the dog will recognize and accept his subordinate role. And surely the gun dog that shares a family environment typically will be happier and better adjusted than the dog quartered in a kennel run.

So despite the dissenters' insinuations of ruination, I firmly believe that sharing the old homestead is the best policy for successfully raising a gun dog. A sure thing in life is pretty rare, but where your gun dog's concerned, there's no risk to keeping your dog indoors.

In the ideal doghouse, length and width should always take precedence over height where winters are extreme. This English pointer's shorthaired coat makes him susceptible to frigid temperatures, and his house could be sized down a bit. Photo © Bill Buckley/The Green Agency

7

In the Doghouse: Outdoor Kennel Essentials

If circumstances permit, your gun dog is much better off sharing life in the house with you and your family. Still, as we all know, circumstances don't always cooperate. You might plan to have your pup live indoors, then, at nine months of age, his overly large size or exuberant personality—or both—suddenly dictate a diametric change of plan.

To keep your sanity, as well as your marriage and family intact, strategically withdrawing your gun dog to a backyard kennel sure beats being dogless. Whatever the reasons, if the gun dog you've bought or plan to buy must live outdoors, housing him properly should be a major consideration.

Just any old doghouse won't suffice. At a minimum, a proper doghouse embodies four main ingredients to meet standard needs as a protective shelter in a variety of weather conditions: It must be draft-free in winter; constructed to allow ample ventilation in summer; large enough to be comfortable; and small enough to retain an adequate percentage of the dog's body heat in cold weather.

Where winters tend to be extreme, the proportion of inside space to the dog's size is critical. Length and width should always take precedence over height. An old fallacy holds that a dog should be able to keep his head upright while sitting in a doghouse. Actually, a dog enjoys greater security and comfort in the reclining position. Correctly proportioned, the house should permit the dog to be most comfortable lying down, while still holding his head fully upright without touching the ceiling. If the dog can sit up straight, then the house is too big to be effectively warmed by his body heat in cold weather.

Drafts can be easily eliminated by a baffle that's higher than, and diagonal to, the entry port. By making the baffle easily removable, you can increase air circulation in hot weather. And, stressing air circulation, raise the doghouse base approximately three inches (8 cm) above the ground to allow cool breezes to enter and help prevent dampness that causes mildew and floor rot. An ordinary brick laid flat under each corner of the doghouse accomplishes this nicely.

In regions of wide temperature variation, insulation shields against winter cold and, when combined with suitable ventilation, tempers summer heat. It's not difficult to find doghouses for sale with built-in insulation, as well as fittings for hot weather ventilation. Doghouses with double floors, with or without insulating material in between, add increased protection against long cold spells.

Unfortunately, the design of some doghouses seems less concerned with practicality than with catching the buyer's eye and fancy. Foremost are those with cathedral-like peaked roofs that substantially increase the interior space, thereby reducing the ability of the dog's body heat to warm it properly. Perhaps lacking in visual appeal, a flat, sloping roof nevertheless economizes inside space to make better use of body heat. The roof also functions as a convenient spot where a dog can rest comfortably in the sun. Fitted with hinges, the roof can be lifted to clean the house's interior.

The entry door need only be big enough to permit the dog comfortable access. Too large a door will allow excessive cold air to enter in winter, along with rain and snow on blustery days. Of course, rain and snow can be deflected by an overhang above the entrance. In winter, nailing a piece of heavy canvas or carpet over the opening adds additional protection against wind, rain, and snow, as well as prevents escape of the dog's body heat.

For those handy with tools and wood, it's a snap to custom design and build precisely the kind of doghouse you want. There are many books available on the subject for those searching for guidance. But even less-handy owners should have no difficulty obtaining commercial, prefab doghouses with a wide range of features to meet their needs. These vary from the most basic shelters to near mansions, with all the comforts and conveniences short of hot-and-cold running water. Since you'll obviously pay more for frills, careful, knowledgeable shopping is important.

Besides conserving body heat more efficiently than a cathedral-type roof, a flat, sloping top also functions as a convenient spot for your gun dog to lie down and soak up some sun. Photo © Lon E. Lauber

Nothing beats a clean, well-kept kennel facility when your gun dog can't share indoor quarters with you. Right now, this kennel run and doghouse dwarf its intended resident, a tiny eight-week-old golden retriever pup. But he'll grow into it pretty quick. Photo © Lon E. Lauber

Naturally, where you shop is a matter of choice and personal convenience, but there's no shortage of commercially made doghouses available through canine specialty catalogs, pet shops, hardware outlets, and even garden centers. So, if you simply shop around a while, you should eventually find the doghouse you like and the one that best suits your dog's needs.

After finding an appropriate doghouse, where and how you place it will be critical to your dog's comfort, health, and well-being. Face its entrance in a southerly or easterly direction to take advantage of the best weather year-round. Of course, the seasons play an important role in placement. In summer, for instance, shade, for at least a portion of the day, becomes vital. Especially from midday on, shade from tree cover is essential. Lacking natural shade, dark-tinted, fiberglass panels placed over the doghouse and kennel run will provide an artificial alternative, so, too, will a tarpaulin strategically draped over part of the kennel run.

During the months of heavy winter snows, of course, the panels or tarpaulin should be removed to avoid collapse and possible injury to your dog.

Cleanliness should be observed at all times, no matter what the season, but it is absolutely essential in summer. Eliminating fleas, or at least controlling them, requires a regular schedule of disinfecting your dog, his house, bedding, kennel, and yard. Be sure to include some fresh bedding inside the doghouse in which your dog can comfortably nestle.

One of the best materials for summertime dog bedding is cedar, either in shavings or chip form. Not only does it deter fleas, it also imparts a clean, pleasant aroma to the kennel dog's coat. For winter use, since it helps hold body heat well, ordinary straw is among the best and cheapest bedding materials.

Proper kennel yard sanitation is equally important at all times. Twice daily removal of droppings, along with weekly disinfection of the kennel yard, keeps parasitic infestation to a minimum.

When circumstances conspire to keep your gun dog in the doghouse, at least make sure he's comfortable. Then resolve not to neglect him merely because he's become an outside resident. Freely share your time and yourself with him, and you can retain part of the indoor closeness lost to kennel living.

The collar and lead are the two most vital elements for training and controlling your gun dog. This springer pup wears a slip or choke chain training collar for his SIT lesson. Photo © Alan and Sandy Carey

8

The Collar and the Lead:
The Primary Link

The collar and the lead are the two most fundamental items needed to successfully begin training a gun dog. Consider how futile it would be to try to establish any sort of control over your dog without a collar and lead. Obviously, then, the right combination deserves careful selection.

Unfortunately, puppies are often the victims of unsuitable collars and leads. Sometimes inexperienced owners buy improper collars or leads, while other times, owners stick new puppies with hand-me-downs from long-departed family canines. Poor-fitting, stiff, leather collars paired with weighty, steel-link leads initiate pups to slave-like restraint. It is no small wonder that so many puppies rebel at the basic link connecting them to their owners. It is no less surprising that some dogs never do become fully adjusted to the apparatus.

APPROPRIATE COLLARS AND LEADS
The six-to-ten-week old puppy's first collar and lead should be made of the lightest material obtainable, yet they should still provide secure restraint. Soft, flat nylon-braided collars that let the buckle seek its own hole, or the single-ply nylon-web type, are light, supple, and long-lasting. These are better choices than even the narrowest leather collars. A ten-to-twelve-week-old puppy will be nicely matched with a six-foot (1.8-m) lead of half-inch (1-cm), single-ply nylon. Heavier collars and leads will be needed as your puppy matures.

When the dog is fully-grown, a variety of different collars can be considered. One option is the slip or "choke" collar that most professional trainers use. A collar that tightens or loosens depending on the tension applied, the choke collar optimizes control for the most effective training results. Valuable as it is for training, a choke collar left on an unsupervised dog can be a definite safety hazard; it should be removed immediately following a training session or a walk. Slip collars come in leather, nylon, and plastic, though the metal-link version is the most popular. The correct size will readily slide over a dog's head and ears, leaving a couple inches (5 cm) of slack.

In addition to a training collar, your dog will need a collar for everyday wear. These can run the gamut from various grades of leather to nylon, to other synthetics, and to metal links. Some collars even utilize a mix of materials. Expense aside, for an everyday collar on an adult dog, I prefer leather. High-quality leather, given reasonable care, has roughly the life expectancy of the average gun dog, and both mellow at about the same rate. As for styles, collars that are flat, round, or partially flat (rounded on one side and flat on the other) are available, with the round type favored for longhaired breeds, and the flat kind favored for shorthaired dogs. The partially flat variety is appropriate for both coat types.

Most gun dog owners shun the garish assortment of colors available and instead opt for the more traditional brown, black, or natural shades. The hunter-orange collar is one practical exception. The reflective strip makes a dog far more visible day or night, should he accidentally get loose and run the road.

A brass identification plate engraved with your name, address, and phone number can easily be attached directly onto a flat collar. Round collars, however, require the use of an "S" hook to hang a tag. Ordinarily, this is a fine enough arrangement, but the tag can sometimes catch and tear loose in brush. A partially flat collar circumvents that possibility altogether, since, as with the fully flat collar, it permits attachment of an identification plate to the leather portion. In any case, whatever your dog's collar type, such identification should never be overlooked.

The lead is the other important tool needed from the very beginning. For training, the perfect lead to go with a choke collar is made of either single- or double-ply nylon in three-quarter-or one-inch (2- or 2.5-cm) width—the latter for larger breeds such as German shorthairs, Labs, and Chessies. For utility-training purposes, a twelve-to-fifteen-foot (3.5–4.5-m) lead is adequate.

However, your utility-training lead normally won't prove practical

Your name, address, and phone number engraved on a brass ID tag firmly attached to your dog's collar will greatly assist, but not guarantee, his return if he gets lost. Photo © Kent and Donna Dannen

for general use. You will also need a lead appropriate for your dog's daily walks. If you walk your dog near auto and pedestrian traffic or other dogs, a sturdy four-foot (1.2-m) lead will guarantee tight control while not excessively restricting your dog's movement. Facing less busy conditions, a standard six-foot (1.8-m) lead will suffice. Your choice of materials ranges from double-ply nylon to heavy plain or braided leather. Leather leads can be flat or round.

Although it is not uncommon to use a dog's everyday collar in the hunting field, concern for safety begs against it. However slight the possibility that a tight-fitting collar might hang the dog up on a wire fence or in heavy brush, it is advisable to eliminate all risk. The best insurance for this is a rollover or safety collar, the kind with an O-ring in the center. Since the O-ring lies flat on the dog's neck, like the rest of the collar, the entire unit can easily roll over if hung up on wire fences or heavy brush, keeping it virtually snag-free. Choosing one in hunter-

orange will also make the dog more visible in thick cover.

Leads for field use offer wide choice. Short field leads keep a dog close at heel when going from cover to car, but longer, multifunction leads have their place, too. For example, a longer half-leather, half-chain lead handily hitches a dog to a fencepost or tree while you lunch or take a rest break. With link chain forming the lead's lower half, the dog won't attempt to chew through it.

Another variety, called the Jaeger lead, features several metal rings sewn into eight feet of choice-quality leather. Strategically placed, the rings make length adjustments possible and allow you to loop the lead around your neck and under your shoulder, leaving both hands free. The Jaeger utility field lead is one of my favorites.

The buckles and rings on collars and the snaps on leads vary significantly in quality and strength. Bypass hardware made of cheap pot metal and spend a bit extra for solid brass or nickel-plated steel. Quick-release snaps are simply a matter of personal preference. Bolt snaps, which incorporate a spring-accuated rod similar to a door bolt, are universally conceded to be the strongest and most dependable type.

Lastly, but of utmost importance, is getting a correctly sized collar. A collar fits properly if, when in place on your dog, you can comfortably slide two fingers under it. Specific instructions on determining the proper-sized collar for your dog are found in most canine specialty catalogs. You can also use a tape measure, loosely held around the middle of your dog's neck, to determine your dog's neck size.

Using the proper collars and leads will ensure easier, safer, and more pleasurable training sessions, daily outings, and hunting experiences for both you and your gun dog.

This chocolate Lab displays a lightweight, flat collar, matched with a six-foot single-ply nylon lead. Heavier materials will replace these as the puppy grows.
Photo © Denver Bryan

9

Safe Haven: The Crate
for Home and Road

Next to the collar and lead, the dog crate or portable kennel is possibly the most valuable piece of equipment a dog and owner can have. From day one, a crate should become an accepted haven for your gun dog pup, a place where the young dog can retreat from play or overenthusiastic children, or simply sneak off to take a nap.

A crate has no equal when it comes to housebreaking a dog. Used in combination with a regular feeding schedule and prompt outside visits after eating, a crate can greatly facilitate and hasten the housebreaking process. Excluding the unavoidable accidents, most dogs will strive not to soil the "nest," so to speak. Crated at night and whenever unsupervised, the pup will whine, bark, pace, or scratch to warn that he needs to go out. Gobs of praise given each time the dog performs outdoors will eventually instill the proper habit. The fewer the indoor accidents, the faster your dog will become housebroken, and a crate definitely helps to minimize mishaps.

The crate also routinely serves as a comfortable dog bed. Leaving the door open on the crate allows the dog free access while someone's home, but offers confinement, when desirable, to keep the dog out of mischief. Something else to bear in mind: Not all of your guests will be dog lovers. Crates have been credited with saving friendships from time to time.

Certainly, veteran gun dog owners recognize and prize the crate's value for transporting dogs safely to and from the field. Uncrated in a

High-impact plastic or fiberglass crates, like the one this English setter is testing, generally carry economical price tags. Photo © Denver Bryan

Wire and aluminum crates make up the middle price range, and serve adequately for use at home and in autos. With the added visibility a wire-mesh crate offers, both dog and driver enjoy a better view. Photo © John R. Falk

vehicle, a dog can be injured, but worse, an uncrated dog can distract or interfere with a driver, resulting in a bad accident. Confined in a crate, however, a dog can't be a nuisance; cannot be smacked against a seat, dashboard, or gear; and won't deposit drool or muddy paw prints on upholstery. Additionally, a safely crated dog cannot dash out into traffic through a carelessly opened car door, or munch contentedly on gun cases or ammo boxes when unattended.

Should field plans include an overnight stay, a crate answers the need for safe, secure quarters for the gun dog, whether left in the car or lodged in the owner's room. Some motels and hunting camps will allow only crated dogs inside to insure against damage.

Crates are made in a variety of materials and sizes. At the upper end of the price range are the custom-made wooden models featuring top-quality carpentry and polished brass fixtures. The lower price range offers models made of high-impact plastic or fiberglass. Though relatively durable, some of the cheaper crates provide poor ventilation and can be uncomfortable for dogs in hot weather.

Aluminum and wire crates make up the middle price range. Top-of-the-line aluminum models combine lightweight and maintenance-free durability, but close attention should be paid to their ventilation properties.

Possibly, in terms of both price and practicality, the wire-mesh or welded-wire models suggest the logical compromise. Fully ventilated, these crates offer hot-weather comfort and the added option of fitted covers that hold in the dog's body heat during cold snaps. Minus the cover, these crates also allow complete visibility both for dog and owner.

Regardless of their construction material, most crates come with either straight or slanted fronts, the latter to fit conveniently in station wagons. Thus, a crate destined for use both on the road and at home should be chosen with this in mind. From a practical standpoint, doubling up the crate's function makes good sense, since using your dog's normal sleeping quarters in the car will give him a greater sense of security while traveling.

Don't make the mistake of buying a crate based on the size of your six-to-eight-week-old puppy. Base your purchase on how big he'll be at maturity (unless, of course, you decide to buy an inexpensive small crate to take him through his first six months, or so). If your full-grown dog can stand and sit erect and stretch his forelegs straight out while prone, the crate is about the right height and length. To determine the proper width, subtract about eight to ten inches (20–25 cm) from the crate's length.

Conditioning your puppy to his crate is generally no problem, assuming you begin as soon as you bring him home. Make him comfortable in it, and he'll quickly learn to accept it as his own special place.

This seven-week-old yellow Lab happily munches one of four daily meals that nutritionists advise for puppies up to three months of age. Photo © Lon E. Lauber

10

Diet

Ensuring your puppy's proper nutrition will depend on the food you choose for him, as well as the feeding habits you establish. Puppies require about twice the amount of nutrition as adult dogs, since they're growing at a fast rate. But, unlike those of adult dogs, puppies' stomachs are small and cannot handle a large amount of food in a single feeding. So, they must be given several meals daily during their first five or six months.

Nutritionists generally advise that puppies receive four daily feedings from ages six weeks through three months; then, from three to six months, three meals. Between six and twelve months, two meals a day are recommended. Naturally, general advice should always be adapted to each individual puppy and regulated accordingly. Some pups may begin refusing a fourth meal before reaching three months of age. Food intake will depend on your puppy's size, age, metabolism, and activity level.

Chances are the kennel owner or breeder who sold you your pup will provide you with a small sample of your puppy's first food. If you decide to switch to another type or brand, do so gradually, increasing the ratio of the new variety to the old variety over seven to ten days to avoid potential stomach and intestinal upset.

Naturally, personal preference will dictate which type of food—canned, soft-moist, or dry—you choose for your pup. Brand names are also a matter of personal taste; today's major brands are all considered to be high-quality foods, meeting your dog's nutritional needs from puppy to senior.

Always measure your pup's food portions so they can be adjusted as necessary. Measured amounts of food enable you to keep tabs on your pup's overall condition and growth. Some pups need slightly more

An occasional treat, such as a dog biscuit, can serve as a reward for a lesson successfully completed. Photo © Lon E. Lauber

or less chow than others to maintain proper weight and steady growth.

Avoid letting your pup become overweight. A pudgy puppy is not necessarily in prime shape; in fact, excessive weight places undue strain on bones that are still soft and growing, and can lead to abnormalities.

It is equally important that you maintain a regular schedule for your puppy's feedings. Not only will this contribute to proper digestion of meals, but it will also prove vital in establishing the housebreaking routine, which depends on regularity, in concert with trips outdoors fifteen to thirty minutes after each meal.

A clean bowl of cool, fresh water should always be available to your puppy. Adequate water intake is necessary to the assimilation of food and to your puppy's good health. For the sake of convenience, your puppy's water bowl can be kept beside his food dish.

Since dogs are creatures of habit, they thrive on routine. For this reason, it is a sound idea to keep your pup's food and water bowls in one place and to feed him there, regularly.

11

Socialization and the First Steps of Training

YOUR PUP'S FIRST DAYS AT HOME

Of most immediate importance on your new puppy's homecoming is getting settled in comfortably. With food, water, and a proper place to securely bed down all taken care of, the next most important step in converting your puppy into a happy, well-adjusted, and useful prospective gunning partner is socialization. How your puppy integrates with all that surrounds him, his total immediate universe—his perspective on life, as it were—depends in great measure on how he relates to you and your family.

During his first few days at home, your pup soaks up experiences like a sponge. Everything your puppy sees, hears, and smells becomes basic knowledge. The pup needs gentle guidance—subliminal at times— to encourage and channel learning in the right direction, the direction *you* want the puppy to go.

During those first few weeks in his new home, your pup imprints on you and other family members—a step critical to his proper development. Recognizing his name and quickly becoming aware of and accepting his niche in the social structure of the family, much as a wolf does in the pecking order of the wolf pack, is of utmost importance for your pup. Properly socializing him is the only way to ensure that happens.

The more time you spend playing and romping with your puppy, the quicker and more completely he'll adapt. Simultaneously, he'll be building his trust in you and confidence in himself, thus molding the foundation needed for his future formal training. While your pup is taking in his surroundings, you should start monitoring—surreptitiously—that the experience he accumulates leads to good habits and proper, normal behavior.

Early in his socialization, your pup should receive no explicit correction efforts or punishment. But it is advisable to think ahead of your pup, to try to anticipate what he's liable to do. Then, if the anticipated action is undesirable, steer him in a direction you'd prefer. What this amounts to is distraction in advance, a technique most mothers cultivate quickly after raising a couple of kids.

Getting conditioned to the environment of your household's sights, sounds, and smells becomes a paramount part of your pup's socialization. Never baby your pup or consciously alter your normal routine to accommodate him. Since he must learn to live with the sounds of family life, don't attempt to shield him from the ordinary rattle of pots, pans, and dishes, the wail of the vacuum cleaner, the stridency of TV commercials, and the cacophony of what the kids call music emanating from their boomboxes.

Apart from excessively rough treatment or openly mean handling of the puppy, your youngsters should be encouraged to indulge in regular play sessions with him. Actually, if your children are old enough, they can and should become involved, at least part-time, in your pup's daily feeding, grooming, and exercising. That will not only acquaint the pup with being handled by persons other than you, it will teach your youngsters a keener sense of responsibility.

In summary, your pup's early socialization should emphasize the positive aspects of his subconscious learning experiences, conditioning him to fit naturally into your daily life and preparing him for the serious obedience and formal field-training lessons yet to come.

TEACHING BASIC COMMANDS

The terms you use in acquainting the puppy with proper and expected behavior are an important part of his learning. I say "terms" advisedly; they won't be commands at first, only guideposts until their meaning is fully understood by the pup. Those terms include: NO—the one he'll hear ad nauseam—HERE or COME (your choice), SIT, STAY, KENNEL, and the release mechanism, OKAY or ALL RIGHT, to let him know he can resume normal activity. Let's start off with the basics.

Before anything else, a pup must learn to recognize his call name.

The start of a beautiful friendship for you and your new gun dog puppy begins with his proper socialization. Fresh from his first trip away from Mom and littermates, this English setter pup isn't sure he's having fun yet. Photo © Denver Bryan

This should precede any command. Also, whenever completing an order, the term ALL RIGHT or OKAY should be used to release your dog to continue with whatever he was doing.

HERE is one of the most crucial terms in establishing control of your pup. When learned properly, this command reestablishes to your pup that you are the boss. It enables you to correct, to reinforce, and to redirect your dog's actions. To teach it to your pup, squat down on one or both knees; after calling his name and saying "Here," begin delightedly clapping your hands. Heap on the praise and patting when your pup does come to you.

If he comes part way and hesitates, continue clapping your hands and start moving away, while again calling "Here," and encouraging him to follow. For really hesitant pups, a food reward, such as a bit of liver or chunk of hot dog, can start him coming briskly when you call. Once the habit takes hold, simply substitute praise and petting for the

Youngsters (under adult supervision) should be encouraged to indulge in regular play sessions with a new puppy. Here a basketful of springer pups get a joyful hug from a little guy. Photo © Dale C. Spartas/The Green Agency

tidbit.

SIT is probably the easiest term to teach. Either of two methods is effective. A food treat serves as a useful tool for method number one. Holding a goodie just out of reach above the puppy's head, move the snack back toward his rump. While intently following your hand's movement, without realizing what's happening, the pup will involuntarily fall back into a sitting position. As that occurs, call his name and say "Sit." Then give him the treat along with praise for his performance.

For the second technique, a pup must be thoroughly accustomed to a collar and lead. With the pup collared and leashed, get his attention by calling his name. Then, lead in your right hand, tug straight up as your left hand pushes downward on the pup's rump while telling him, "Sit." Again, praise him profusely and let him know how pleased he's made you.

STAY is one of those terms that some people teach as an integral part of the SIT command; in other words, when the dog is told to SIT, he must also STAY in that position until released, which is as it should be. But used independently, STAY is an important, useful command. It offers the flexibility of ordering the dog to refrain from leaving an area—a room, car, or kennel—or merely to remain in a specific, previously ordered position, such as to sit or lie down.

Teaching STAY requires patience and repetition. Try placing your pup in the kitchen, then block the doorway as you call him by name and say "Stay." Each time the pup attempts to exit the doorway, pick him up, place him back in the room, and say "Stay." The same training method works in a car, or kennel, or wherever. Simple repetition and praise for obedience will ultimately prevail.

KENNEL is a handy term; it is in effect a synonym for "Enter." Use it whenever you want your dog to get inside something: his crate, a vehicle, a room, etc. Of course, the word kennel, itself, suggests the starting place for teaching the lesson. Initially, every time you place your pup in his crate, tell him, "Kennel." He'll soon come to know the term and readily obey, since his crate, or kennel, is a safe, comfortable, friendly place that he trusts. Later on, whenever you take your pup out in the car, use the same KENNEL command to have him hop in. At first, you may have to assist him; eventually, as he grows, the order will be the only help he needs.

GETTING YOUR PUP USED TO A COLLAR AND A LEAD

Your puppy's first taste of restraint, other than your hands, will be his collar (See chapter 8, "The Collar and the Lead: The Primary Link" for appropriate types). Since your puppy must learn to live with his collar, the sooner you put it on him, the better off both of you will be.

At first, your puppy will demonstrate instant dislike of the collar by sitting down and trying his best to scratch it off. Try to distract him by getting him to play with a ball or some other toy. But fairly quickly, he'll realize that the collar's still in place and start scratching at it again. Once more, distract him, and keep distracting him until he forgets the collar altogether. Don't remove your puppy's collar; make him wear it all the time.

The best method for getting your pup used to the lead is the direct technique. But before breaking him to lead, let him become thoroughly accustomed to his collar. Usually a day or so is sufficient. Then, attach your lightweight lead to your pup's collar and get ready for action. He'll balk and jump around immediately. Let him battle it briefly, then

After learning to recognize his name, this springer spaniel pup gets some lessons in SIT (opposite page, top), *HERE* (opposite page, bottom), *and HEEL* (above). All photos © Alan and Sandy Carey relinquish all tension, allowing him to feel only the slight weight of the lead. Still giving him total slack, for a minute or two, permit your pup to lead you wherever he wants to go; then tighten the pressure again. His rebellious antics are sure to follow, but keep the tension on the lead a little longer each succeeding time before relaxing it.

Continue this exercise at least three or four times daily for about ten minutes each session. Your pup should be completely lead-broken by the second or third day.

ACCLIMATION TO CAR TRAVEL

Sometime during the third week after you bring your pup home, and after he's well acclimated to house and family and collar and lead, you should begin getting him well acquainted with the car—and riding in it. Make this a gradual procedure, sitting with him in the car for brief periods two or three times a day, without even starting the engine. When your puppy seems to accept the car as a friendly place, turn on the engine and let it idle while he becomes used to the sound. Continue the drill every day until the engine noise doesn't phase him; then take him on a short ride, maybe a mile (1.6 km) or so, to get him used to the car's movement. Gradually lengthen those rides over the next several days, after which your pup should be okay for travel. From this point on, whenever you take your pup for a drive, put him in his crate, for safety's sake and to condition him to traveling in it. Also, as a precaution against carsickness, schedule your rides far in advance of your puppy's next feeding.

12

Whistle-and-Hand Signals

Virtually everything we do in our daily lives hinges on communication. It enables us to understand and to be understood; through communication we learn and also enlighten. Without it we would barely function. Communication is just as vital in the process of training a dog. By sound and sight, we communicate to our dogs what it is we want and expect of them. Sounds—our vocal commands—are rudimentary in most early training. Those sounds become progressively more meaningful through inflection, volume, and tone. When enhanced by body language—the sight cues—sounds strengthen comprehension and help nourish the partnership evolving between dog and owner.

Many times in the hunting field or on the marsh, however, occasions arise when vocal orders cannot be heard. Audible sound must then be combined with sight cues to communicate. These are the times that require whistle-and-hand signal combinations to convey your instructions.

You use the whistle to first get the dog's attention and then to set him up to receive the hand signals. Communicating by whistle has obvious advantages. Effective over long distances, the sound of a whistle, once fully understood, is an imperative, even more forceful than a shouted order. Similarly, the hand signal, especially over a distance, is frequently more recognizable than a spoken command. Thus, by combining whistle and hand signals, hunter and dog can effectively stay in contact regardless of field conditions.

Unquestionably, the epitome of such communication occurs between hunter and retriever. Without whistle-and-hand signals, even the most proficient fetch dog would be significantly hampered. When using the signals, however, you can demonstrate effective teamwork and the most efficient system for gathering virtually all downed game, in-

Whistle-and-hand signals make up the all-important communication link between handler and dog in the field. Here a springer spaniel is schooled in the combined whistle-and-hand signal to HUP, or SIT. Photo © Bill Buckley/ The Green Agency

cluding a high percentage of cripples that would be lost otherwise.

Whether retriever, spaniel, or pointer, and regardless of age, your dog can begin to learn some whistle-and-hand signals. Whistle signals can be defined in three ways: 1) to stop the dog from whatever he's doing and rivet his attention on you for another command; 2) to send the dog on or in a new direction; or 3) to call the dog in. Begin to accustom your pup to whistle signals during his daily routine. For instance, at suppertime, blow a short blast to halt him and grab his attention for further orders. Then beckon him to his dinner, whether outdoors or in, with a long trill of the whistle, the customary RECALL or COME-IN signal.

BASIC WHISTLE-AND-HAND SIGNALS

Undoubtedly, the most indispensable whistle command is the short blast compelling your dog to halt, whether in a standing or sitting position, as appropriate to his breed or type. Teaching this command is relatively simple. If your dog's already obedient to the SIT or HUP command, merely work in the whistle with the verbal order, and eventually exchange it for the latter.

Begin with your dog walking at heel on a lead. Stop and tell him to sit; then immediately blow a single whistle blast. If he doesn't sit at once, tug directly up on your dog's lead and simultaneously force him into the sitting position by pushing his butt to the ground. Repeat the lesson, and gradually substitute the whistle for your verbal order until your dog sits solely on the whistle.

Subsequent whistle training will require you to modify your signals to correspond with your dog's breed. The clipped, piercing whistle blast, for instance, should cause your spaniel or fetch dog respectively to HUP or SIT, but it directs your pointer to WHOA in a standing position. Trilling is the universal COME-IN signal for all types of gun dogs, as is the double toot to RESUME HUNTING, or, with accompanying hand signal, to CHANGE DIRECTION.

Hand signals cover a wider variety of commands that can be used in close, as well as at medium to long distances. In ordering your dog to SIT, use the extended arm and flattened palm in a kind of waving-goodbye motion. Commanding your dog to DROP or LIE DOWN is done by extending your arm straight out and pointing your index finger downward as you pump your forearm up and down.

To teach LEFT, have your dog sit facing you about fifty or sixty feet away, and toss a retrieving dummy to the left, using your left hand and arm in a somewhat exaggerated motion. Blow a short whistle blast to anchor him. Then, command OVER, using your dog's name as you simultaneously double-toot your whistle and fully extend your left arm in the direction you want to send him. For greater emphasis, you can also take a stride or jump to the left at the same instant.

Obviously, to send your dog to the right, throw the dummy with your right hand and take an extra step in that direction as you relay the whistle-and-hand signal to him. Continue these drills, lengthening both your distance from the dog when you begin, as well as how far you toss the dummy, until he performs perfectly every session.

From these exercises you can progress to hiding the dummy, which should be scented with the extract of the main game bird you intend to hunt. Make sure to plant the dummy out of sight of your dog and off to one side, so your dog can't trail your scent to the dummy drop. Your goal here parallels the previous training drill, except that this time your dog will not see the dummy thrown and must rely only on your signals to place him close enough to the unmarked (blind) fall to find it by scent. To save time, plant more than one dummy in each direction, spaced sufficiently far apart so that the dog can be worked separately on each without confusion.

When your dog has gotten the hang of these blind rights and lefts, begin working him on the GO BACK command. Signaling a retriever or spaniel to GO BACK is very important. If he's too short of the bird's fall on a "blind" retrieve or on a poorly marked bird, his pattern must be extended by signaling him to GO BACK, which really means to GO OUT FURTHER. Eventually you will give him a mixed bag of retrieves to complete under your whistle-and-hand signals.

How much and how fast you can progress depends not only on your pupil, but on how frequently you can work with him. Many short exercises always accomplish more than two or three prolonged ones. RIGHT, LEFT, HUP or SIT, and GO BACK are best accomplished through formal drill in a good-sized, open field.

Types of Whistles

Although all whistles make noise, enough variations can be found to make choosing one a matter of some importance. Many Europeans and

This ten-week-old Chesapeake Bay retriever puppy is learning to HEEL. Once the pupil shows good progress, the whistle will be introduced along with the vocal command. Photo © Lon E. Lauber

The most popular whistle is the police-type, utilizing a pea-sized cork. It enables a hunter, like this one, to produce a varied assortment of blasts and trills that are easily distinguished by the gun dog. Photo © Denver Bryan

some spaniel owners favor a staghorn whistle. These are often made with two whistles of very different tone, one on either end, and are advantageous if you decide to train your dog to more than the customary variety of field signals.

By far the most popular whistle is the police-type, utilizing a pea-sized cork that lets you create an assortment of diverse blasts and trills that are easily distinguished by your dog. The Acme Thunderer and the Roy Gonia brands are two of the best known and most widely available of the police-type whistles. Plastic is best, since, unlike metal, it won't stick to your lips in frigid weather.

When selecting a whistle, avoid the so-called "silent whistle." Dogs can pick up the high-frequency sound such whistles produce, but being unable to hear the sounds himself, an owner can't possibly duplicate the variety of signals needed to work his dog properly.

Whatever kind of whistle you select, buy two. In fact, it's not a bad idea to buy two each of two different kinds and hang them on lanyards. And if you're the least bit forgetful, buy a couple of spares to keep in the car.

13

Learning to Fetch

Some breeds—and certainly some individuals within breeds—manifest a stronger and earlier desire to fetch than others. The instinct to fetch usually shows itself very early in the retriever breeds, a little later in spaniels, and still later in some of the pointing breeds. You must take into account such characteristics when selecting appropriate fetch-training techniques for your dog.

THE TWO BASIC FETCH-TRAINING METHODS: AN OVERVIEW

The natural training method of retrieving relies on artfully channeling strong, natural fetching instincts into the pattern that will best serve the gun. Something of a misnomer, the natural training method is not totally devoid of force. On the other hand, the late bloomers (and the ones who seemingly would never get it on their own) are the best candidates for the force-training method of retrieving. As its name implies, the force-training system employs "force," meaning coercion rather than physical force, ranging from fairly mild to stern. For the dog, this is a no-choice system, requiring him to retrieve on command, every time, whether he wants to or not.

Some experienced retriever and spaniel trainers recommend that all dogs be force-trained to retrieve, citing the occasional refusals to fetch by dogs taught via the natural method. Others disavow that philosophy, contending that the natural training method produces happy, enthusiastic retrievers, as opposed to desultory, mechanical workers. I tend to support the force-training school, primarily because of its reliability.

PLAY LEARNING

Whichever method you employ, you must begin with "play training" or "play learning." What is play to the pup and you is actually a combined learning and teaching experience; the pup is learning and you are teaching, though informally. Play learning really begins the moment you first bring your puppy home. Everything the pup sees, hears, and smells accentuates learning, whether it is "taught" or merely experienced by osmosis, so to speak. Earlier, I referred to this process as socialization. Play learning is a continuing part of the pup's socialization, his association with you as the pack leader.

In the leader role, you channel or guide your pup's learning without any form of discipline other than an occasional "No" to steer him away from unwanted behavior. Begin your pup's retrieving play in a long, narrow hallway with minimal distractions. Place his crate behind you at one end of the hall. Then, let the pup scout out the environs to his satisfaction. Make sure he's completely at ease before starting the game.

Now, introduce your pup to the dummy, which for now can be an old cotton sock (wool hunting socks are too abrasive), glove, or large handkerchief knotted several times to give it bulk. Let the pup sniff and mouth it, but not run off with it, until he's sure it's an okay thing.

Then, skitter the dummy enticingly around on the floor to get the pup excited and eager to catch it. When he's totally interested, toss the dummy four or five feet in front of him. As he bounds over and picks it up, call him by name and enthusiastically tell him "Fetch." From your squatting position, tap your leg to encourage him to bring the dummy back to you. Ninety-nine times out of a hundred, he won't bring it directly back to you, but will try to run by you and get to his crate, his "safe haven." However, you'll be blocking his way. Reach for his collar and gently guide him to a full stop. Do not try to take the dummy from him; merely hold him in position while you sweet talk and pet him profusely. Let him enjoy holding the dummy for a few minutes, as he relishes your soothing hands and your voice telling him what a great puppy he is. Sooner or later, he'll relinquish the dummy to you. Just don't try

Retriever breeds, like this young Lab, usually show a strong, early instinct to fetch. Proper training strengthens and guides that instinct to useful purpose in the field and blind. Photo © Bill Buckley/The Green Agency

Fetch training should begin with "play learning," best started in a long, narrow hallway or alley, free of distraction. Later, backyard sessions begin. Photo © Alan and Sandy Carey

With satisfactory progress, such as this ten-week-old golden retriever demonstrates, you can switch your pup over to a regular puppy dummy for fetch training. Photo © Lon E. Lauber

to rush it. Repeat the whole sequence two or three times, then quit, while he's still eager for more. You don't want to risk boring him and having him lose interest in this new game.

How often should you play this game with your puppy? Every day if you can manage it, but at least on alternate days. Keep gradually increasing the distance you toss the dummy—as long as the pup continues progressing satisfactorily. After a few weeks, you should switch from your improvised dummy to a regular puppy dummy. Once your pup is used to the new one, you can try relocating your sessions to your backyard. If you've done everything right and have a pup with a truly strong desire to retrieve, the transition should go smoothly. Always bear in mind that these are play-learning exercises. No discipline, no punishment, only repetition—and withholding of praise when things don't go right. The serious, formal retrieving comes later, when the pup is mature enough and has built complete confidence and trust in you.

GETTING WET

Concurrent with play-learning to fetch, your retriever or spaniel pup needs to learn that water is good for swimming. Becoming familiar and comfortable with getting wet all over is a significant and necessary part of the lifetime work of every retriever and spaniel. This is equally true for the versatile, or continental, breeds, while not so critical for the other pointing breeds, whose water work usually proves incidental. However, an early introduction to water can be beneficial in later field work for most any breed of gun dog.

Although it shouldn't be a difficult or complicated process, a puppy's first water entry too often becomes a traumatic ordeal. The inexperienced owner's usual blunders include not paying attention to water temperature, choosing a less than ideal location, and impatiently rushing the procedure.

Warm weather and warm-to-slightly-cool water provide a good start for your pup's introduction. Let's face it, no matter how often you may do it, jumping into cold water ain't much fun. Now, think how much of a shock it would be to a puppy experiencing it for the very first time. Talk about trauma.

In addition to warm water, you will need to find an appropriate spot for training. A small, shallow pond or lake with a gently sloping, sandy or gravel bottom, where you can wade safely and easily, makes a good location. A shallow, slow-moving stream is another option, one about forty-five or fifty feet wide, also sloping gently from both banks, with a sand or gravel bottom.

The last third of your successful formula involves patience. Too many owners, subscribing to the old adage, "sink or swim," unceremoniously just throw their pups into the water. They think the quick, direct approach is best to accomplish their goal. Sure, every pup will swim instinctively—to save his life. But the sheer terror he feels at this sort of introduction to water guarantees he won't soon care to dive in again. You need to make swimming a pleasant experience for your pup, strictly fun and games. Getting wet all over for the first time will leave a lasting impression on your pup, and a favorable experience will go a long way toward helping your dog reach his full potential for future hunting.

To begin, just amble along the bank, casually walking in and out of the water in no particular pattern. Talk happily to your pup while encouraging him to trot into the water with you. Go a bit deeper each

Every retriever and spaniel pup should learn early that water and swimming add up to fun. By getting into the water himself, this owner can entice his young Lab to do likewise. Photo © Bill Buckley/The Green Agency

time. If he's reluctant to get in up to his belly, you'll have to cajole him a bit by going a little deeper and praising him effusively for whatever effort he makes to join you. Your job is to see that your pup begins thinking of the water as a fun place to be. However, do not—repeat: DO NOT—toss anything into the water for your puppy to retrieve. At this juncture, retrieving should have no part in your pup's learning to accept and, hopefully, love the water.

A majority of retriever and spaniel pups will take to the water naturally and quickly, as will most of the versatile breeds. Of course, there are bound to be exceptions, and with these dogs, patience and perseverance—the bywords of dog training—must be practiced with faith.

If your pup proves to be one of the exceptions, a water-shy individual, a number of possible solutions can be tried. If a boat is available, try rowing slowly away from shore and, saying nothing, hope your pup will follow. You are trying to make the pup think you're going to leave

A shallow, warm-water pond forms the ideal venue to promote a strong love of water, as this fifteen-week-old Chesapeake attests. Photo © Lon E. Lauber

him. The anxiety of losing you will often overcome his fear of water, and he will get right in and swim after you. However, if the pond is too small, the pup may decide to run the shoreline around to the opposite side rather than swim out after you. Dogs are smart—even puppies can sometimes figure two steps ahead of us. Find a bigger pond before you try this approach.

A variation of the "making-puppy-think-he-may-lose-you" method can be played out effectively in a small, relatively shallow stream. Walk along the bank and, without any words of encouragement, cross the stream without looking back. Your pup may hesitate, but, again, rather than being left behind and risk losing you, he'll usually follow quickly. Make a tremendous welcoming fuss when he catches up. Eventually, doubling back and recrossing the stream once or twice should solidify the experience.

Getting a hunting buddy to bring along his older retriever or spaniel to your chosen pond or stream is yet another way to help the water-shy gun dog. Hopefully, when the veteran dog begins gamboling around in the water, your pup will join in and forget his cautious attitude. If

116

necessary, both you and your buddy can also get into the water with his dog, all the while talking happily and excitedly, to entice your pup to get in and become part of the fun.

If your pup steadfastly refuses to get soaked and swim despite your best efforts over several weeks, you'd be well advised to trade him in on a new model, except, perhaps, in the case of one of the traditional pointing breeds. I know it's a lot easier to give that advice than to accept it, but no matter how attached you may have become to the pup, if you really want a hunter and not just a house pet, ask the breeder to swap him for another pup. A retriever, spaniel, or versatile pointing dog that is water-shy isn't worth fooling with as a hunting dog.

THE FORCE FETCH

As mentioned, there are degrees of natural retrieving instinct, depending on breed and, often, the individual dog. Force training is more appropriate for some breeds, particularly ones that are slow to catch on. The gun dog that is "force-trained" to retrieve does so because he must; it has become part of his job. Once properly schooled in it, he can be relied upon to fetch all the birds you kill cleanly and, almost without exception, the cripples as well. Force training, however, is usually a tedious series of lessons that once begun should be carried out to successful completion. To quit along the way invites the dog's probable future refusal to fetch at all

To begin force training, you will need a six-foot (2-m) lead, a chain, a leather or nylon choke collar, a twenty-five- or thirty-foot (7.5- or 9-m) check cord, and some sort of retrieving dummy. In addition, the "training table" has achieved widespread popularity in recent years for teaching pointing dogs to WHOA and for the early stages of force training to retrieve. The average training table is about eight feet long with a ramp on either end for the dog to walk up. A regular picnic table can be used just as effectively, however. What the table essentially does is elevate the dog to a more convenient position for the trainer. Also, when a dog is off the ground, he is somewhat insecure and much more inclined to concentrate on his owner and the lesson at hand. A table is, of course, not mandatory; it is simply more convenient.

With your dog standing broadside to you, if a pointing breed, or sitting broadside to you, if a spaniel or retriever, place the dummy in his mouth and command "Fetch." You'll probably have to open your dog's

A springer spaniel is drilled in the force-fetch retrieve. Trained by this method, a gun dog fetches because he must, and, thus, becomes a reliable full-time retriever under all circumstances. Photo © John McGonigle

mouth by pressing his bottom lip against his teeth with your left thumb. Keeping your left hand under his muzzle, order him to "hold" the dummy, repeating the command each time he tries to get rid of it. Reinforce your command by tightening then releasing the choke collar. Once your dog complies and holds the dummy for fifteen or twenty seconds, tell him "Give," and pour on the praise when he releases it into your hand. Keep these sessions to no more than ten or fifteen minutes daily for as long as necessary to achieve proper performance.

In between these lessons, have your dog hold the dummy and carry it while walking at heel. This five-minute exercise will generally strengthen not only his *willingness* to hold the dummy but his *desire* to do so as well.

Next, you must teach your dog to reach for the dummy at your FETCH command, instead of you placing it in his mouth. To do this, hold the dummy directly in front of his muzzle and tell him "Fetch." He may not respond, in which case, some persuasion—force—must be used. This consists of what is commonly known as "ear pinching," done by grasping his ear and pinching it between your thumbnail and middle fingernail. It's only a momentary discomfort for the dog, but enough to make him open his mouth so you can slide the dummy quickly in as you give the FETCH and HOLD order. Release the pinch as soon as he obeys and heap on the "good boys."

A gradual lengthening of the distance you make the dog reach for the dummy will reward your patient efforts and also indicate your progress. As the lessons continue, you should encourage him to start reaching down at your order. Remember: Brief but frequent sessions and patient perseverance are the keys.

Now, the really tough part. You must make your dog pick up the dummy off the ground—hey, that's where the birds will be after all. There are variations on the best method. The one I prefer is the one detailed in my book, *The Complete Guide To Bird Dog Training*. Let me quote it here:

Place a pair of bricks broadside down on the ground, leaving roughly half a foot [15 cm] of space between them. Lay your dummy, in bridgelike fashion, across the bricks. Now, lead your dog right up to the dummy and tell him to "fetch." Chances are he won't obey the order. While pinching his ear, push his head down toward the dummy and don't relinquish either pressure until he takes it in his mouth. Then make him hold, or even carry while walking at heel, for a minute or two before commanding him to GIVE. Repeat this four or five times at each session.

Arriving successfully at this phase, all you have to do is get your dog to fetch the dummy off the ground at a reasonable distance and bring it to you. Using a check cord to prompt his delivery over increasing distances will prove the final stage of his force-retrieving lessons. All that remains is alternating dummies with freshly killed pigeons or game birds in your sessions. As always, consistency, repetition, patience, and perseverance will eventually produce the desired results: a gun dog that will reliably retrieve what you shoot.

Training on live game birds can be expensive, but ordinary pigeons make ex-cellent stand-ins for the real thing. Photo © Bill Buckley/The Green Agency

14

Pigeons: Game Bird Substitutes

In these days of scarce game birds, lower limits, and fewer opportunities to hunt, is it possible for an aspiring, young bird dog to get enough live-bird training and experience to qualify him for his job? Getting your dog sufficient work on live birds would certainly be a lot easier if 1) you devoted an entire open season solely to his training and eschewed your own shooting sport, and 2) you could manage to hunt him four or five days each week during that season.

Without question, this would prove the very best way for any young dog to gain solid experience on wild birds. Frankly, though, even for the most dedicated bird dog owner, the self-denial and staunch resolve involved would go well beyond the normal call of duty. Fortunately, a far less painful alternative exists. All you need are some live pigeons, a check cord, a blank cartridge gun, a few acres of land, and your eager young bird dog.

Where can you get live pigeons? They're not as difficult to find as you may think. Try commercial or hobby breeders, live poultry markets, and farmers, who will sometimes either trap them in their barns for you or let you handle the job yourself. Wherever you get them, pigeons usually sell at very modest prices, far less than bobwhite or coturnix quail.

For your dog to get optimum benefit out of training with live pigeons, you should know how and where to plant them, as well as what to expect when your dog first encounters them. For a pointing dog, introductory training with pigeons—or with any planted birds—involves two main considerations. First, the birds must be tightly planted; in other words, each one must stay put, exactly where it is planted. Second, you must realize that locating a planted bird presents no easy task for an inexperienced young dog.

A tightly planted bird leaves little to none of the peripheral scent that a wild one normally deposits in moving about. Moreover, the distracting human scent that unavoidably exists in any bird planting situation compounds the challenge even further. That's the bad news. The good news is that working a young pointing dog on a tightly planted pigeon has a double benefit. Besides permitting maximum search time to find the bird, it sets up ideal circumstances for the dog to establish a staunch point, because the pigeon won't be skulking off or flying away. Nothing so incites a young dog into breaking point as a running bird, whereas one sitting tight promotes staunchness.

Learning how to prepare a pigeon for tight planting isn't difficult. Before heading for the field, though, it's advisable to practice and perfect your technique in an enclosed area to avoid having too many pigeons escape. Here's the simple procedure. Holding the bird breast upward in your right hand, tuck its head as far as possible under its right wing with your left hand. Slightly increasing pressure with your right hand will keep the bird's head properly in place while, with your left hand, you cross a few of the bird's primary feathers, in scissorslike manner, over its right foot. Dizzying the bird by swinging it in a circular pattern, and then reversing direction for about ten seconds, further insures that the bird will stay put. That's all there is to it.

An ordinary burlap bag, secured with a piece of string, will do nicely to carry your training pigeons to the field. If you prefer, a wire mesh carry cage, specifically designed for transporting pigeons or quail, can be used. Either one can serve to handle up to a dozen pigeons.

After releasing your dog in the field, be sure he's well out front, with his attention diverted elsewhere, as you prepare to plant a pigeon. When you're certain your dog won't see you, place a bird in an appropriate piece of cover and pull or tuck some grass over it. Alternatively, you may wish to leave your dog in the car while you plant two or three pigeons. Until you're adept at quickly preparing the birds for planting, this is the more practical choice.

Always be sure to diversify your plants, putting them in all types of cover you normally encounter in a day's hunt. Dogs quickly learn to associate the same surroundings with a specific act. If the dog is used to finding a bird in one particular place, he may begin to automatically point that spot whether it holds a bird or not. This can lead to a bad habit of false pointing.

Getting maximum benefit out of training with live pigeons involves knowing how and where to plant them. This owner, preparing to work his pointing dog, makes a "tight" pigeon plant in an open field. Photo © Bill Buckley/The Green Agency

After a pigeon has been successfully planted, whistle your dog in and work him into the wind in the general area of the bird. The object is not to guide him straight to the bird, but merely to start him in the right direction and let him find the plant on his own. If you're not sure he'll point the pigeon, snap a check cord on his collar before casting him off, so you can WHOA him if he tries "busting" the bird—in other words, jumping in to try to catch the bird.

Once he's reliably staunch on all the pigeons he finds, start trying to steady him to wing and shot. If you've got a helper to flush and shoot the pigeon, it will free you to do the check cord "Whoaing" when your dog breaks point at the flush. If you're on your own, flushing and shooting the bird while also handling the check cord can seem to present a perplexing problem. But it can be done. Try planting a pigeon near a tree, which will enable you to pass the free end of the cord around the tree, keeping it slightly slack while you walk in to your dog's point. Then, as you flush the bird and your dog breaks to chase, hauling back on the cord will apply the proper constraint—from behind the dog—to hold him in check.

If wide-open, treeless fields make up your training area, try using a sturdy, but lightweight, pointed metal rod. Roughly twenty-four inches (61 cm) long, the rod should be bent sharply at the top like a cane handle. Shove the rod into the ground deep enough to withstand the sudden lunge of a hefty bird dog. Then quickly slide the check cord under the handle and use it in the same way you'd use a tree trunk. Naturally, the rod must be grounded behind the dog after he establishes point.

Cursed with only two hands, simultaneously working a check cord and trying to shoot a pigeon during these training sessions can really test one's mettle. When I enjoyed the hawklike eyesight and instant reflexes of youth, shooting a lightweight, 28-gauge scattergun one-handed simplified the situation. Oh, I missed a few, but the system worked well enough.

Some folks solve the problem by creating a lasso-like loop in the check cord and slipping it over their head and under one arm. Then, with both hands free and the pigeon airborne, you can still check the

Oops, this pigeon is wide awake and ready to flush if the young English setter on point even twitches an eyelid. But, with the dog in full chase, that is the time to fire your blank pistol. Photo © Bill Buckley/The Green Agency

dog from chasing, though you'll have to be prepared for the jolt when he hits the end of the cord and you yell "Whoa." Of course, if you don't intend to shoot your training pigeons, you can use a blank cartridge pistol and eliminate the entire problem.

The value of live pigeons goes far beyond basic training of young pointing dogs. Pigeons provide extra bird work for fully trained pointing dogs, too. Inexpensive substitutes for game birds, pigeons are excellent stand-ins for correcting bird dog behavioral errors and problem situations, and serve well as a preseason refresher course for a rusty veteran. Thus far, we've only dealt with pointing dogs. Pigeons are equally useful in training spaniels and retrievers to be flushing dogs. There are some differences in method between the two breeds, however.

As we've discussed, for basic pointing dog training, pigeons are planted tight to encourage staunch points. For spaniels and flushing fetch dogs, points (either momentary or extended stops) are to be discouraged. All gun dogs will point to some degree; the pointing instinct is a natural pause in the stalk, just before pouncing on the prey. However, flushing dogs, at least on this side of the Atlantic, are expected to bore in immediately on their birds and put them to flight.

Tight plants for flushing dogs, therefore, would be counterproductive. Instead, you want to encourage aggressive flushes. Two progressive procedures are generally used. The first involves clipped-wing pigeons, birds from which a few primary feathers are pulled or clipped short from one wing. This limits the bird's ability to fly, and sometimes enables the dog to catch it at the flush. It's important that the young dog catch some pigeons in order to promote aggressive or hard flushes from him.

The second method uses dizzied, but full-flighted, pigeons, which can be tossed lightly into cover, such as fairly tall grass or brush. Dizzied birds will generally stay where they're tossed for several minutes, at least long enough for your dog to find and flush them. Using full-flighted pigeons at this stage provides realistic hunting conditions with birds your dog can't catch.

Now, if your young dog has yet to be exposed to gunfire other than blanks, give the pigeon plenty of range, with the dog in full chase, before shooting. The dog should be so intent on following the bird that he won't notice the gun going off. Let him retrieve the pigeon, but don't be in too much of a hurry to take it from him. A few moments to trot around with the prize in his mouth will serve as his reward.

Surely, the bygone era of nearly inexhaustible numbers of game birds—when a gun dog could literally teeth on wild birds a football field's distance from the back porch—will never return. Even so, in today's overcrowded, complex, urban society, we probably should count ourselves lucky that we still have such things as bird dogs . . . and an inexhaustible supply of pigeons to make sure they keep their title.

Increasingly, today's retriever breeds fulfill a dual role as fetchers of waterfowl and flushers of upland birds. Here, a yellow Lab puts up a squawking rooster pheasant out of a snowy field for a pair of gunners. Photo © Mitch Kezar

15

Turning Fetchers into Flushers: Retrievers in the Uplands

Today's retriever breeds, acquired more for their versatility than their specialization, have admirably met the challenge to adapt. In addition to their regular waterfowling duties, they convincingly pinch-hit as flushing dogs when hunting pheasant, grouse, woodcock, and quail in the uplands.

Smaller bag limits and shorter duck seasons have made it impractical for most hunters to keep a dog strictly for waterfowl work. Keeping two dogs, one for waterfowling and the other for upland gunning, poses an even more impractical situation, both from the standpoint of expense and the need for different training techniques.

Inescapably, our Labs, goldens, and, to a lesser extent, Chessies, Irish and American water spaniels, and the rarer flat- and curly-coated retrievers, have been pressured into dual roles to survive as hunting dogs. That most of these retriever breeds can become credible upland bird hunters, given supplemental training and opportunities to gain on-the-job experience, has saved their bacon.

The retriever turned flushing dog hunts much like a spaniel, quartering ground in back-and-forth sweeps, seeking birdy objectives, to the front and sides of the gunner while never drifting beyond shotgun range. Maximizing both body and foot scent, a retriever must pinpoint his quarry, boldly push into the cover, and aggressively put the bird to flight.

Exactly when and how a retriever should begin learning this additional role depends to a large extent on the hunter's chief interests. Most purists frown on less-than-perfect behavior and performance in their dogs' waterfowling duties. In addition, some hunters participate seriously in licensed retriever field trials. Both types of hunters contend that a retriever should be fully skilled in his basic specialty before introducing him to upland hunting. For those espousing such exacting standards and beliefs, there can be no argument. Yet, the average hunter, who's essentially concerned with enjoying a variety of bird shooting with his fetch dog, would be needlessly wasting valuable time by adopting such stringent standards. Since this hunter's goal is far short of flawless field-trial performance, he'd be a lot better off giving his dog an early introduction to the uplands. And that can be started concurrent with the puppy's informal fetch training, simultaneously combining both learning experiences much like spaniels are schooled.

Like any other hunting breed, your young retriever pup needs suitable impetus to trigger his inherent desire to search for game, and that will come only through providing him with as many field outings as you can possibly manage. Every time you get your pup into covers likely to produce game, you'll be fueling his natural enthusiasm for the hunt.

Like his play-fetch training, those early field trips should be viewed strictly as fun and familiarization; the serious stuff comes later. Just let him mosey along, keeping him in front of you as much as possible. When the dog begins using his instincts and his nose to hunt up dickey birds, bunnies, and whatever else he can find that is not too big to intimidate him, encourage him. Pretty soon he'll discover, to his utter delight, that finding, flushing, and chasing critters is great sport.

When he's a bit older and has begun his formal lessons, you can follow up with more serious field training. This should coincide with the dog's dependable obedience to voice, hand, and whistle commands. When, with any of these three means, you can stop, sit, turn, and recall him, you'll be ready to transfer this same control into the uplands.

At this time, you can also begin teaching your dog to be selective about what he hunts, finds, and flushes. Every time he works and pushes up a stink bird (a nongame bird such as a lark, sparrow, etc.), give him a short, sharp whistle blast, immediately followed by a hand signal and double toot to send him in the opposite direction. Only when he works on, and eventually puts up, a game bird or a pigeon you've planted should you whistle-stop him, fire your blank gun, toss a dummy to fetch, and call him in to receive some enthusiastic praise and petting.

Once your retriever is hunting game birds in earnest, keeping him within gun range will almost certainly prove your greatest challenge. Any of several different methods can be used to solve the problem. A

Given proper training and sufficient opportunities on game, most retriever breeds, like this black Lab, can be expected to turn in successful performances as pinch-hit flushing dogs in the uplands. Photo © William H. Mullins

fifty- to seventy-five-foot (15–23-m) check cord attached to your dog's collar and left trailing along as he hunts is often an effective method. Whenever the dog begins working hot bird scent and suddenly forges ahead, showing every intention of exceeding reasonable range, grab the end of the cord and SIT him by whistle command. If he ignores your whistle, simply haul back on the check cord and stop him in his tracks.

You should be aware, however, that except in open or very light cover, working with a long check cord has been known to provoke language strong enough to defrock a clergyman. Continually twisting around and snagging on brush, a lengthy cord can soon frustrate both you and your dog. However, some of the solid-core check cords in braided nylon are stiff enough to help alleviate the tangling problem.

Other range-restricting devices can also be employed to rein in the truly bullheaded fetcher. For instance, you might fasten a three-and-a-half-foot (1-m), medium-to-heavy chain to his collar and allow it to drag between his legs while he's hunting. A piece of rubber garden hose substitutes nicely and does the same job of slowing the dog's pace and

A golden retriever enjoys a rest break during a pheasant hunt, while hunters discuss tactics for the next foray. Photo © Denver Bryan

forcing him to stay closer to the gun.

In addition, another less-awkward contraption to slow your dog resembles an Argentine cowboy's *bolloderos*. It includes two lengths of plastic clothesline, one somewhat shorter than the other, dangling from a snap that attaches to the dog's collar. A three-inch (8-cm), sponge-center rubber ball is affixed to the end of each line. When positioned on the dog, the ball on the shorter line hangs a couple of inches (5 cm) off the ground, while the other drags about six to ten inches (15–25 cm) of slack. As the dog runs, the weighted lines swing freely, twisting around his front legs just often enough to impede his normal gait and slow him down, effectively reducing his range.

Such mechanical range-limiters do offer help in solving this frustrating problem. But the best solution will come from the firm, certain control you should establish through obedience to hand, voice, and whistle signals. Brief, but frequent, sessions drilling your dog to respond immediately to your SIT order, no matter how near or far the dog is from you, will make the difference between an enjoyable hunt and an aggravating one.

After attaining the necessary control of your retriever in the uplands, maintaining his enthusiastic interest will depend on providing him with frequent hunting opportunities and sufficient game contacts. If grouse, woodcock, pheasants, chukars, quail, or other game birds are not always available, ordinary barn pigeons work well. The important thing is to get your retriever as much experience working in cover as possible. Keep polishing his handling and command responses, and you will be rewarded, eventually, with a retriever-flush dog that's doubly more useful and productive than either a waterfowl specialist or a skilled upland bird dog.

The best times to exercise your gun dog are early morning and late evening during hot summer months. Brisk walks make good beginnings. Photo © Kent and Donna Dannen

16

Conditioning Your Gun Dog for the Hunt

Subject to human frailties, we all tend toward procrastination. Somehow the old adage, "Never put off till tomorrow what you can do today," seems to have done a complete turnaround in modern society.

Nowhere is this truth more evident than in shaping up a gun dog, physically and mentally, for the approaching hunting season. Blame it, perhaps, on the lethargy that is summer. But, we all—well, most of us, anyway—seem uninspired to embark on a canine conditioning program before fall's first chill.

Because there are no shortcuts to properly conditioning a gun dog, a late start means working a tight schedule. Under ideal circumstances, it takes about eight weeks of increasing exercise for a dog to reach peak condition. Fortunately, though, worthwhile results can be achieved in as little as four or five weeks.

The first step in getting your dog ready for field work should be a visit to the veterinarian. Take along a fresh stool sample from the dog to be checked for worms or other parasites. Also, have the dog tested for heartworm and given updated shots, as well as receiving a complete physical examination. Then, after getting a clean bill of health for your dog, you can start working him back into top hunting shape.

A good conditioning program should provide the dog with the right kind of exercise in the appropriate amount to help drop surplus weight, firm flabby muscles, improve lung capacity, increase endurance, and toughen pads. Accumulation of extra weight between hunting seasons afflicts most hunting dogs. And the only way to a trim, fit physique is to combine a properly balanced diet and a calorie-burning exercise routine.

Much as we fashion our own individual exercise programs and match them to our age, weight, and lifestyle, so, too, should these factors be applied to conditioning a gun dog. The sensible program, therefore, calls for progressive moderation. Start your dog's workouts slowly, increasing their intensity and duration in small increments.

Your own individual circumstances will largely influence where and how to begin. Weather forms the key element. A July or August start for your conditioning program, no matter where in North America you live, means that temperatures will be scorching by midday. Obviously, this indicates early morning and late evening as the best times for workouts, with the cooler morning hours preferred.

Field exercise, running freely as he would while hunting, is the best conditioning for your dog. Extra advantage can be realized if your dog is fitted with a device known as a "roading" harness. Attaching the added weight of the roading harness for the dog to drag will help build up his muscles and endurance. The extra weight generally consists of about three feet of heavy-link chain hooked to each side of the harness via a couple feet of shock-absorbing rubber strap. Roading harnesses, in leather or heavy-ply nylon, are available from several commercial outlets.

Although there are a number of devices for conditioning gun dogs, most of them prove impractical and expensive for the one-dog owner. Among them are treadmills, much like the ones used for stress testing and indoor exercise of health-conscious humans, and tractor-mounted outrigger bars capable of exercising four dogs simultaneously.

There are, however, more mundane alternatives. In the initial stages of conditioning, when overexertion must be avoided, brisk walks are especially worthwhile. Walks of fifteen to twenty minutes, twice daily for the first week or so, will develop a solid foundation for your dog, leading to a longer, more rigorous exercise form.

Swimming, which is an excellent supplement to other activities, offers still another alternative. Recognized worldwide as one of the most beneficial kinds of exercise, swimming, as a gun dog conditioner, provides an extra benefit: It can be performed even on the hottest summer afternoon. That makes it both practical and pleasurable, cooling off your dog while enhancing his lung capacity and muscle tone. Moreover, you can extend your dog's exercise periods, if the water site is large enough, by having him swim along behind your rowboat or canoe.

You can extract yet another dividend from swimming by tossing

A yellow Labrador retriever enjoys fetching a dummy from the cool waters of a pond. Swimming is great conditioning exercise, and combines training work as well. Photo © Lon E. Lauber

retrieving dummies into the water for your dog to fetch. Not only will this provide exercise for your dog, it will also help keep his marking abilities well honed, and your control of him sharp. And while these sessions will be especially beneficial to retrievers and spaniels, pointing breeds will benefit as well.

Biking or jogging while your leashed dog lopes along with you presents another good alternative. However, there are possible safety risks. Loose-running dogs along the route can create problems, especially if your dog is excitable or feels threatened. Automobile traffic, other bikers, and joggers also pose potential distractions or safety concerns. Yet, biking and jogging should not be overlooked as valuable conditioning tools.

When biking or jogging, choose a lightly trafficked route. Start your dog on ten-minute jaunts, four or five times weekly, working up to fifteen-minute sessions over the next eight to ten days.

Safely controlling a dog from a bicycle can often prove challenging. There is, however, an accessory on the market that offers a viable solution. Called the K9 Cruiser, it attaches directly to a bike's rear wheel. Its

Every conditioning program should also include a training refresher course.
Here, an English setter's SIT command is reviewed. Photo © John R. Falk

sturdy, metal, outrigger-like bar is fitted with a twenty-four-inch (61-cm) lead that keeps the dog safe and fully controlled. After a short acclimation period, most dogs readily take to trotting alongside their owners' bikes.

Whichever conditioning exercise you choose, if properly implemented, it should enable your dog to run without tiring for at least three-quarters of an hour by the end of the fifth or sixth week. Then, unless opening day is really breathing down your neck, just continue to prolong those outings by a few minutes each time.

During any conditioning session, always carry an adequate supply of fresh, cool water for your dog, this is especially important in warm weather. Never him get overheated. Also, remember to carefully monitor exercise time to avoid overexerting your dog.

Although time consuming, conducting a training refresher course concurrent with your conditioning program makes good sense. Ridding your dog of those mental cobwebs acquired during the offseason and getting him back on track is also critical to field performance. The best procedure is to start right at the beginning with a review of basic yard training.

Of course, your dog should already know and promptly obey all of the fundamental commands: SIT, STAY, HERE, HEEL, and WHOA (or, in the case of a flushing breed, HUP). But even for the most obliging pupil, a quick refresher course should sharpen and refocus his attention.

Equally important is a review of your dog's responses to hand, voice, and whistle signals in both the yard and the field. During his first few hunting trips, your dog should be leashed and run through a few yard-training commands, just to remind him that you're still in charge.

Only by investing the required time and effort in advance of the hunting season will you be able to go into the field confident that your faithful partner is ready for the hunt.

17

When the Road Beckons: Canine Needs for the Upcoming Hunt

It can take substantially more time and planning than may first be imagined to get properly organized and fully equipped with the essential canine hunting gear for fall weekend hunts. And "putting it off till tomorrow" can frequently skewer an otherwise promising and eagerly anticipated outing. Much of the requisite equipment must be ordered from canine specialty catalogs, where the fulfillment time can often exceed four to six weeks on certain items—one more reason why advance planning is never a bad idea.

If you're driving a station wagon or 4x4 vehicle, a crate or barrier device will likely form the centerpiece for transporting and possibly sheltering your gun dog through an overnight (or longer) hunting trip. Of course, you could allow your dog complete freedom in the car, for both traveling and sleeping overnight. But for his (and your own) safety and comfort, it doesn't make good sense—and it surely puts your vehicle's upholstery at risk.

If you elect to install a wire-mesh barrier that confines the dog to the area behind the back seat, you will lose space otherwise available for baggage and other gear. Besides, rattling around in all that extra room, your dog could possibly injure himself during quick stops or sharp turns. The more practical option is some sort of carrying crate, as discussed in chapter 9, "Safe Haven: The Crate for Home and Road." These portable kennels provide safe, comfortable transport for dogs, and they also

A car crate affords the most comfortable and safest place for transporting your gun dog. With a ruffed grouse already in hand, this hunter and his English setter are ready to hit another cover. Photo © Bill Buckley/The Green Agency

double as snug overnight quarters to keep a dog secure and out of trouble.

Some motels permit hunters' dogs to bunk with them. In those instances, a portable kennel makes an ideal dog bed. With its door latched, your dog is safely confined, avoiding all chance of accidents involving the carpet, drapes, or bed. Moreover, a crated dog is more likely to remain quiet in the room, especially if you keep the TV set turned on softly while you're out grabbing a bite.

Water is of paramount importance for any hunting trip, not only for drinking but for pouring over a dog to avoid heat exhaustion. Although streams or ponds, which enable a dog to immerse himself and lose excess body heat, are readily accessible in many areas, water is not always handy at rest stops. Carrying a one- or two-quart canteen of fresh water in your vehicle effectively circumvents the drinking problem for both you and your dog.

How can your dog drink from a canteen? Some can manage the task. But an easier way is simply to fashion a dish of sorts from a fifteen-inch (38-cm) strip of aluminum foil, which can be carried folded flat in your pocket. An alternative to the foil is a regular-sized Ziploc plastic bag. Just pour in some water, hold the bag wide open, and let your dog lap away.

When hunting in arid regions where water is scarce, carrying along an adequate supply of your own water is mandatory. Intense heat and dry conditions are tough on hunters, but are much worse on their dogs that have to cover about ten times more territory in an average day. Even in less arid places, having your own water supply is good insurance. For cooling purposes, a five-gallon can filled with cold water is generally sufficient to pack in your vehicle. Then, when you return to your car between hunting covers, pour a generous amount over your dog's body, especially the underparts, to cool and refresh him.

Another of the most important items on any hunting trip is a complete canine first-aid kit. Good kits are available from several of the canine-specialty mailorder houses. But if you choose to make up your own, it should include tweezers, a small scissors, one roll each of one-inch (2.5-cm) and two-inch (5-cm) gauze bandage, one roll each of one-inch (2.5-cm) and two-inch (5-cm) adhesive tape, a dozen three-inch-square (8-sq-cm) gauze pads, a half-dozen cotton swabs, a small bottle of 3 percent hydrogen peroxide, a small tube of 2 percent yellow

There is no drinking problem for this vizsla, who has quickly learned the technique of slaking thirst from a handy canteen. Photo © Jim Schlender

oxide of mercury, a small bottle of boric acid, and a small bottle of sterile, distilled water. An equally important adjunct to the first-aid kit is a pocket-sized, basic first-aid manual. Assuming you're not a doctor, premed student, or other medical professional, the manual will prove invaluable should the need for prompt first aid arise. Make sure the book is indexed for ready reference and printed in large type for easy reading with or without glasses. It would not be a waste of time to become reasonably familiar with its contents and to review them periodically.

In addition to the standard first-aid items, consider including in your kit a pair of long-nosed pliers for removing porcupine quills. Quill removal can be difficult and is always highly uncomfortable for the dog. But the procedure can be mollified in a couple of ways. First, because porcupine quills are hollow, cutting them in half tends to collapse the quills and make them easier to remove. Also, soaking the quills in a mixture of one cup of vinegar and two teaspoons of baking soda (other potentially useful items to bring along) is effective. Two to three appli-

The quill is definitely mightier than the sword for this German wirehaired pointer after an unfortunate encounter with a porcupine. Some gun dogs learn quickly to avoid "porky" contact. Photo © Denver Bryan

144

cations spaced four or five minutes apart will soften and shrink quills for quicker, less-painful removal.

A good, practical field lead is another must article on every gunning trip. You'll need one whenever you walk your dog at highway rest stops and when taking him from car to hunting cover when he's fresh and eager to hit the ground running. I've never found a more practical field lead than the Jaeger model described in chapter 8. This design allows you to tether your dog to a tree, post, fence, or car bumper, while you enjoy lunch, coffee, or a rest break.

If you bell your dog, bringing along a spare is smart insurance. If the first bell somehow gets detached and lost, an extra will spare you lots of frustration when you're trying to keep track of your dog in heavy cover. Not too many folks who use beeper collars for their dogs will own two beeper collars, so a spare is probably not an option. Instead, make a point to bring along a dog bell, just in case your beeper batteries quit. Of course, that's cause to remember to pack a spare battery.

Dog boots certainly are a sound investment, too. If sand burrs or cactus infest the areas you usually hunt, you are, or will quickly become, aware of the need for a couple of pairs of properly fitting dog boots. In addition to prickly ground cover, dog boots can be just as valuable for those times your dog suffers sore, tender pads that otherwise might take him out of action for several days. Good boots often enable sore-footed dogs to continue hunting without major discomfort or damage.

Disdained by some hunters, a flushing whip is less a symbol of authority or cruelty than it is a useful field tool. Besides its primary bird-flushing function, a whip makes a handy, short field lead to keep your dog close at heel and to briefly prevent him from hunting. Several varieties of flushing whips are available commercially. My personal preference is the J.A.S.A. Flushing Whip, a round-handled, leather whip some twenty-seven inches (69 cm) long.

Other items of importance are the various implements required for the necessary post-hunt grooming of your canine hunting partner. If your dog sports a medium- to longhaired coat, he'll likely need a brisk brushing to eliminate caked mud, sticktights, burrs, and twig bits accumulated during the day. To do the job efficiently, you'll need a stiff-bristled brush, a combination coarse- and fine-toothed metal comb, a stripping comb, and, more often than not, a mat breaker to get through the really messy tangles.

Thankfully not too big for his boots, this English pointer will continue to hunt, despite tender pads. Photo © Bill Buckley/The Green Agency

Following the grooming, you may have to put your first-aid kit to use, tending to any cuts or scrapes not noticed earlier. Your first-aid kit's boric acid solution can be used to flush out any foreign matter, including weed seeds that may have collected in your dog's eyes. A jar of foot-toughener, such as Tuf-Foot or Pad-Kote, will come in handy to relieve bruised, tender pads.

Eventually, after all your other chores are done, it'll be time to feed your dog. And on the road, your dog's food and water needs are even more crucial than at home. No matter what his routine maintenance diet is, your dog will need more calories to offset the extra energy expended working long hours in the field.

If you've already started him on a high-protein regimen during his preseason conditioning program, fine. But, if not, besides larger portions of his regular ration, your dog will require some higher protein food, such as meat, to keep his energy at peak performance. That, of course, means your pretrip rations should include a can of meat for each day you'll be away, as well as enough dry or soft-moist dog chow (plus a small emergency supply, just in case you run short).

Naturally, you can't forget your dog's food and water bowls, nor, for that matter, should you neglect to bring a can opener and a fork or spoon to dole out canned meat and mix with his dry meal. And, even if a ready supply of fresh water is anticipated, bringing your own is a good precaution. At the very least, you'll need some water while on the road to and from your destination. A clean plastic milk jug or soda bottle with a screw-on top will serve adequately as a water carrier. But, if something a bit more elegant appeals to you, a picnic jug or canteen can be used to carry water for you and your dog while on the road and in the field.

Beyond the already mentioned essentials, your own list of weekend canine hunting gear can be increased or condensed depending on your personal needs and experience. Over time, which itself may have contributed to my own forgetfulness, I have come up with a gilt-edged solution to combat the "Damn it, I forgot to bring it!" syndrome. It's a container, prepacked with such essentials as a can opener, fork, spoon, spare collar, dog bell or beeper, food and water bowls, grooming items, dog boots, and a first-aid kit. I do admit to forgetting *the kit* on a couple of occasions. But, I'm sure they were times when I forgot to ask my wife not to forget to remind me not to forget my prepack.

Owners of well-trained gun dogs become amazingly popular with nondog-owning friends during the season. But, specific rules of conduct for dogless companions must be observed. Photo © Denver Bryan

18

Field Etiquette for Dogless Hunting Companions

Sooner or later, as a gun dog owner, you're going to become popular with gunners not fortunate enough to have their own gun dog. Most of these underprivileged souls will jump at the chance to hunt with you . . . and your well-trained gun dog.

In fact, you may be surprised—no, shocked—at the lengths some of these hunters will go in trying to extract hunting invitations from you. Hints of World Series box seats, connections for fifty-yard-line Super Bowl tickets, even disclosing secret fishin' spots may be the inducements dangled enticingly in exchange for some canine field companionship. All well and good; enjoy and take your pick.

But bear in mind, however, that many of these folks, though enthusiastic, may have little or no experience hunting with dogs. And you can't afford to excuse certain behavior from your guests, because of ignorance or inexperience, that could be detrimental to your dog's training and deportment in the field.

There are some very specific rules of conduct involved. The most basic one is simply that your invitee behave like a guest—in other words, act courteously, unassumingly, and take his cues from you, the host. But since it's easy for anyone unaccustomed to having a dog around to be forgetful of the dog's presence, constant vigilance must become your watchword. You'll have to force yourself to be alert to, and to anticipate, the most common mistakes dogless hunters can make.

For instance, a guest won't endear himself to you if he thoughtlessly slams a car door on your dog's tail or foot. Nor will said guest win brownie points by heedlessly opening that same car door at a busy highway rest stop if the dog is uncrated in your vehicle. Ditto for accidentally letting your dog flee the car at one of your tiny, but always productive, bird covers. Such mistakes can only guarantee your guest's banishment from future hunts.

Inexperience is sure to spawn other transgressions, and you should try to guard against them. Take this sequence: You and your guest, Frank, are about twenty-five yards (23 m) apart, following your young Brittany, Jacques. While quartering the field up front, Jacques suddenly jumps a cottontail from a grassy clump and takes a few hesitant steps in pursuit. Immediately, Frank shoulders his gun, ready to zap the bouncing bunny. But, fortunately, your warning shout comes in time to prevent his shot. *You* know that bird dogs should have no truck with rabbits. But Frank doesn't know it. From Jacques' earliest training, you've painstakingly dissuaded him from chasing cottontails, and he's become practically bunny-proof. Yet, if Frank had shot that rabbit right in front of Jacques, a single trigger-pull might have destroyed months of training progress.

Consider another possibility for courting disaster, this one comprised of several blunders: Exiting the woods, Frank sights Jacques pointing staunchly in midfield. Excitedly yelling the news to you, he runs out full tilt toward the dog on point. Unnerved by Frank charging up directly behind him, Jacques reacts instantly, his intense stance markedly softening. Then, with Frank dashing past him to get ready for the expected flush, Jacques suddenly breaks point and your guest shouts for him to "Whoa!" Totally ignoring the order, Jacques races by Frank, only to bust right into the middle of a covey of bobwhites. With birds exploding left and right, Frank zeroes in on a grass-skimmer Jacques is chasing. Two quick, luckily high, misses end the escapade.

You can only shake your head in disbelief at the series of no-nos just observed. First, your guest ran up to a dog on point. Such an action can convince a dog he's done something wrong and is about to catch all sorts of hell. No wonder Frank's charge frightened him.

Approaching directly behind a dog on point was mistake number two. A staunchly pointing dog, concentrating completely on his birds, is apt to be oblivious to a gunner's advance directly to his rear, out of his line of sight. The dog may, therefore, be startled into breaking, or at least, softening his point. The potential problem can be avoided merely by always approaching at a wide angle, so the dog is certain to observe the approach.

Frank committed a third error while trying to undo his previous two by bellowing "Whoa" when Jacques broke point to chase the quail. Without the owner's specific permission, a guest should never issue commands to, or try to control, someone else's dog. Besides, a stranger's orders will probably go unheeded by most gun dogs, anyway. At best, they will only cause confusion.

Blunder number four originated before Frank even started scampering out to Jacques on point. As a guest, going to a point before the dog's owner is far beyond ignorance. Basic courtesy alone should suggest that a guest wait until his host can position himself for a possible shot when his dog is on point.

Furthermore, a guest should never presume to flush the bird in front of another's dog. Tradition directs both guns to move in to the point simultaneously. Customarily, the dog's owner handles flushing chores at the day's first point and thereafter alternates with his companion, thus insuring more-or-less equal shooting opportunities for both guns.

Finally, capping the other five infractions in Frank's string of miscues was popping at a low-flying bird closely chased by the dog. Suppose the dog took a sudden leap up at the bird just as Frank shot. Or what if bird had unexpectedly veered downward?

Perhaps these examples may seem exaggerated. But some of them I've witnessed. And I can state unequivocally that some hunters who lack experience gunning over dogs can transform a promising day into a positive nightmare for a dog's owner.

The worst of these hunters will shoot directly over rock-steady dogs on point. And I've puzzled over why those dogs didn't simply cut and dash nervously back to the sanctuary of the car. Just think how unsettling it must be for a dog, whose hearing sensitivity is about five times greater than our own, to experience a shotgun blast right overhead. It's certainly enough to totally disarrange a young dog and seriously jolt even a veteran.

The litany of mistakes common to the canine uninitiated seems endless. It is hardly unique to observe guest gunners trying mightily to command someone else's dog to retrieve a downed bird directly back to them. Of course, the owner should be made aware of a bird the dog didn't see fall, so he can direct the retrieve. Ordinarily, if a dog is trained to retrieve and sees a bird downed, he'll fetch it to his owner, and a guest shouldn't meddle in the process.

Dogless, but experienced, hunters generally exhibit proper field etiquette. This black Lab's owner knows his buddies are well versed in gunning with flushing dogs. Photo © Mitch Kezar

Despite the potentially onerous aspects of inviting a guest to hunt with you and your gun dog, there is a way other than sheer vigilance to circumvent most problems. Candor right at the outset, appropriately gentled with diplomacy, about the do's and don'ts of canine field etiquette is the best and safest course to follow. Then ask your guest, frankly, about his level of experience hunting with gun dogs, and let him know there's no shame in lacking experience. Tell him you respect and value his honesty. Make him feel comfortable asking you questions about what and what not to do.

Then, if your guest conducts himself properly, courteously, and the day goes well, let him know you'll be happy to invite him along again. And count yourself proud to have groomed a dogless hunter into an enlightened field companion, not only for yourself, but for your fellow gun dog owners, as well.

Pretty, yes, but certainly more than just a decorative appendage, the gun dog's tail has much to tell. This English setter's high tail carriage bespeaks confidence in his location of the quarry. Photo © Mitch Kezar

19

Telling Tails: Why Your Dog Has a Tail and What It Can Communicate to You

From the beginning, sporting literature has reflected humankind's fascination with the tails of hunting dogs. References scattered liberally throughout the writings dependably depict the hunting dog's posterior appendage in dazzling verbiage. Seldom do tails merely "wag"; instead, they "vibrate," "flutter," or "blur." And when are they other than "merry," "jaunty," "lofty," "sky-high," or "ramrod stiff?" In the sporting literary game of heads or tails, it seems the tail always comes out ahead.

Literature has not been alone in fixating on the tails of hunting dogs. Long an object of superstition, tails have inspired almost as much folklore as witchcraft. To assure that your hound stayed close to home, it was only necessary, according to legend, to chop off a bit of his tail and bury it under your doorstep.

So much superstition was assigned to the tails of hunting dogs that it even bamboozled royalty. During the Middle Ages, various monarchs imposed a heavy tax on owners of all hunting dogs with full-length tails. Slicing off a hunting dog's tail, those regents presumed, would disastrously impact his hunting abilities, effectively excluding from the hunt all but the aristocracy who could easily pay the prejudicial tax. Perhaps smugly pleasing to royalty, the docking dictum did diddlysquat to deter the serfs, still ably abetted by their bobtailed dogs in joyfully poaching the gentry's ostensibly protected game.

But whatever its claim to literary and folklore celebrity, the gun dog's tail does indeed provide utilitarian as well as aesthetic value to the hunter in the field. An intrinsic component of the canine anatomy, the dog's caudal appendage, far from being a mere afterthought of nature, serves a definite end use, as well as several secondary ones.

As nature intended, the dog's tail acts essentially as combination stabilizer and rudder when the dog's in motion. Both on land and in water, the dog's tail provides him faster maneuverability. Additionally, whether unaccompanied by, or in combination with, other body movements, the tail functions as an important means of communication between dogs.

The question of whether cropping roughly two-thirds of a hunting dog's tail (a common practice with certain breeds) impairs his maneuverability afield or in the water is one of continuing debate. Owners of "stubbie" breeds, including spaniels and continentals, scorn the notion that lack of a full tail handicaps their dogs' field performance. "Nondockers," however, hold to the traditional contention that no stubtailed breed compares to the full-length tail breeds in grace and agility on land or maneuverability in water. Resolving the issue seems about as likely as snakes growing feathers.

To the hunter in the field, the dog tail's major practical value likewise lies in its role as a dependable signal flag, constantly telegraphing information about the dog's present and anticipated actions afield. Could any message from a dog's tail be more definitive than when he's closing in on nearby game and the blazing hot scent intensifies with each step? Obviously, it's the dog's nose that's sucking in that exhilarating aroma, but it is his tail that fairly shouts what has him on fire. Dispelling all doubt, that tail tells you to turn on the adrenaline and get set for action.

Surely, the message of making game is the most commonly recognized signal conveyed by a dog's tail. But, it's only one message among several a tail can express. Learning how to read these signals will come with experience. And once learned, it takes only a glance to translate what your dog's tail is telling you.

For example, merely by watching a dog's tail, the seasoned eye can instantly determine whether a dog is seriously hunting or just out for a run. No matter how fast and wide the dog, his tail will basically move in quick, rhythmic swings if he's intently seeking game scent, clearly telegraphing a purposeful search. Conversely, slack tail movement plainly says, "Hey, I'm just out here running for the sheer love of it." If that dog's afterburners have kicked in, his tail likely will be carried low and limp. Only a quick shift in direction will momentarily bring his rudder back to life again.

Owners of longtailed pointing dogs can instantly determine if their

Increased maneuverability on land and in water is a valued function of the gun dog's tail. This Labrador retriever uses his strong tail just like a boat's rudder to help steer him in the water. Photo © Alan and Sandy Carey

dogs' points mean a bird that's precisely located or one that's merely nearby somewhere. Tail carriage and movement are the clues. A dog that has his bird pinpointed invariably stacks up rock-staunch, tail stiff, still, and elevated at an angle above his back, consistent with his natural style. On the other hand, perceptible flagging and a sagging tail on point confirms uncertain bird location. Of course, some dogs do flag when pointing released birds, but the dependably staunch dog seldom flags on wild birds—if he's got them nailed down.

Though it's a definite no-no, a rabbit occasionally will draw a point from even the most tried-and-true pointing dog. Caught in the act and painfully aware of their mistake, some old campaigners slowly soften on point, their tails gradually sagging with each step of the approaching gunner. Speech could no more emphatically communicate embarrassment than those sorrowfully slumping tails.

Besides communicating a wide range of meanings in the field, the gun dog's tail also acts as a beacon to keep the gunner apprised of his dog's whereabouts in dense cover. A high, cracking tail, barely seen above tall undergrowth, often provides an owner the only clue to his dog's location. And, when attempting to find a dog on point in such cover, the white tip of that 90-degree-high tail can shine like a light in the dark.

Thus far, it seems tail cues apply principally to gun dogs having full-length tails. But docktailed breeds are not excluded from the "signal corps." Although lacking the flair of the longtails, they nevertheless relay the same information. It's just that their messages are delivered in more soft-spoken tones. An especially perceptive eye may be needed to catch the messages, but, since the stubtailed breeds generally hunt closer to the gun, nothing should get lost in translation. Whatever owners of bobtailed dogs may sacrifice in aesthetics, however, they gain in avoidance of split tails and other accidental injuries that often beset the long-tailed breeds.

Chopped or full-length, the hunting dog's tail is guaranteed to inspire admiration and debate in equal amounts for about as long as there are folks who take to the field with dog and gun. It might be said, this is a tale with no end in sight.

20

A Sense of Smell

The sense of smell in humans has been steadily deteriorating since cave-man days. Over the eons, our nostrils have evolved from the large, flat, flaring, gorilla-like openings of the Neanderthals to the much smaller, downward-pointing ones prevalent today. We can recognize pungent odors—fresh-brewed coffee, bacon and eggs frying, toast burning—but countless subtle smells often escape our notice.

Canines, however, smell a zillion different scents . . . without even trying hard. A look at the average canine nose holds some obvious clues. Those sizeable nostrils, pointing straight forward, are attached to an elongated (in most breeds) muzzle that accommodates millions of ol-factory receptor cells, those little devils that process scent messages for the brain. With such olfactory sensitivity—totally unimaginable to hu-mans—dogs can sift through the myriad odors extant in the world to-day and catalog those of particular significance to them. But this is not so surprising, really, when considering that while sight, sound, and touch predominate in the daily lives of people, a dog's existence revolves es-sentially around scent.

Dogs employ scent in virtually everything they do, from locating food and mates to identifying family and strangers. Don new clothes and a hat—if you ordinarily go bareheaded—and approach your dog downwind from a distance. Even if you've had him for many years, he'll think you're a stranger and bark. Then let him catch your scent and watch his tail wag furiously in recognition. His eyes may fool him, but never his nose.

Remember the contention that a healthy dog has a cool, wet nose? Both the temperature and the humidity (wetness) of that nose contrib-ute substantially to gathering and refining scent for the olfactories to process. It is well documented that dogs with warm, dry noses are far

from keen in scenting ability. In fact, those conditions often indicate that the dog may be sick.

But what exactly is scent, and how does it travel to a dog's nose—or our's, for that matter? Molecules in varying numbers, alone or attached to microscopic particles, make up scent. Different scents may have different-sized molecules and form codes, if you will, peculiar to each thing dispensing it. These codes are invisible, of course, but scent has been variously compared to smoke, fog, and steam in the way it is disbursed.

If all else was constant, scent molecules would most likely either become attached to objects (grass, brush, etc.), be touched by the emanator, or simply drop and remain on the ground. Naturally, though, changes in the environment do occur, and all of them affect scent and its travel. The most profound factors involved are temperature, humidity, and wind.

Ordinarily, for better or worse, it takes a combination of these three factors to influence a gun dog's scenting abilities. Cool, moist air, for example, generally provides half the equation leading to good scenting conditions. The other half comes from soil that's moist and warmer than that of the air. Like metal to magnets, scent molecules, or particles with molecules attached, settle and adhere to damp, warm earth.

However, if the air is warmer and drier than the soil, scent will rise more quickly and dissipate sooner, especially if blown away. Reverse the conditions—air colder, earth warmer—and scent molecules will tend to hug the ground.

Of course, rain quickly washes away scent. Heavy winds diffuse it, while soft breezes gently waft it to high-headed bird dogs. Snow on frost-covered ground provides tough scenting, whereas better scenting conditions exist when snow falls before the ground freezes.

Bright sunshine presages poor scenting, and the combination of hot, dry air, hard ground, and gusty winds form some of the worst possible scenting conditions for a gun dog. Throw in a venue of wide-open terrain, with sparse cover to gather and hold scent molecules left by birds moving through it, and it is even tougher for the gun dog.

Some dogs tend to concentrate more on ground scent regardless of

This English pointer's keen nose has sifted through myriad scents encountered in the field and led him inexorably to his target, a bird well-hidden in the grassy cover. Photo © Denver Bryan

Both temperature and humidity (wetness) of the gun dog's nose contribute substantially to gathering and refining scent for the olfactories to process. Photo © Lon E. Lauber

cover and terrain. These dogs are generally slower, more deliberate hunters since they have to keep their noses close to the ground. The faster-paced dogs that hunt high-headed use airborne scent, the bulk of which comes directly off the bird's body and is carried to the dog on the breeze. But even these dogs will often dip nose to ground when body scent is scarce or when trailing a runner or cripple.

Even when scenting conditions are ideal, if birds are quiet and not moving about, the amount of scent they distribute will be minimal, making them more difficult for a dog to locate. Thus, when your dog hunts diligently, and comes up empty, the situation calls for slowing the pace. Encourage him to hunt closer, to try to pick up some ground scent that may lead him to fresher body scent.

However, even with optimum scenting conditions, there will be times when your dog's nose seems turned off. At such times, other, often unsuspected, elements may be at work. Among the culprits may be medications, food, noxious fumes, or health problems. Some of these are temporary. Tobacco smoke in inadequately ventilated cars, for instance, can briefly impact olfactory sensitivity. Auto exhaust can also seriously impair a dog's scenting acuity.

Some medications are suspected of affecting a dog's sense of smell. Your veterinarian should be consulted about any of these possibilities. Cheese, especially strong types such as sharp cheddar and Swiss, has been accused of putting a dog's nose off, at least briefly. Obviously, that should admonish you from sharing sandwiches containing cheese with your dog while in the field, no matter how pitifully he begs.

Early season hunting also can skewer your dog's smelling efficiency. Just as humans are subject to the discomfort of a high pollen count, so are dog's nasal passages irritated by pollen, resulting in decreased olfactory sensitivity. Heavy cover greenery can also interfere with your dog's smelling efficiency before the first killing frost thins it out.

Even after the killing frost, should very dry field conditions prevail, inhalation of plant debris and weed seeds may temporarily clog your dog's nostrils, obviously altering his scenting ability. Brief fits of sneezing generally signal the problem and alleviate it quickly. But prolonged, continual sneezing or snorting may indicate deeply imbedded debris that requires veterinary attention to dislodge it.

With more in-depth study of scent in its varying forms—its pungency, durability, and dispersion—we may someday unravel its intriguing mysteries. Until then, however, at least recognizing the vagaries of the scenting conditions confronting our dogs should help us understand why they perform so admirably sometimes and so amateurishly at others.

Yet, when all else is said and done, no matter what the season, weather, or conditions, never lose sight of one thing: your dog's scenting ability outpaces your own by about 1,000 to one. Trust his nose, not your own. At his worst, he's a far better hunter than any human, and if you hadn't thought so initially, you'd still be hunting alone.

Often enigma to man and dog, the ruffed grouse always provides a worthy challenge. Experience has taught this English setter to successfully handle those individual grouse that can be handled. Photo © John R. Falk

21

The Grouse Dog

Hunters, especially when gathered together in the informality of a hunting or fishing lodge, perennially generate evening-long polemics. The
subject matters little; from shot sizes to fly patterns to turkey calls to
bamboo versus graphite fly rods, opinions flow unchecked and reti-
cence takes the role of stranger. And although the only acceptable fisti-
cuffs are verbal, these afterdinner "speakers" seldom exude caution, or
lack of conviction.

But no matter how high the bombast, drop in two words, "ruffed
grouse," and, magically, the whole tenor of the evening swaps ends. For
a moment, at least, church could hold session. Reverence? Possibly. But
more like a pall of extreme wariness engulfs the room. The pin dropped,
silence waits tentatively for the rebirth of sound. Yet, even the most con-
tentious know-it-all retreats into extended pipe-lighting, uncontrollable
coughing, or sudden laryngitis. And the truly savvy veterans, shrinking
deeper into their chairs, guardedly toss out only the most vague gener-
alizations, instantly labeled as pure speculation.

Then, when the dialogue focuses, as it eventually must, on which
breed of gun dog consistently scores as the best grouse dog . . . well,
that's when even the most practiced political animal can be ensnared
trying to rebut some artfully calculated observation on an issue of such
hypersensitivity. Fledgling bird hunters in attendance may sit awestruck
and wonder why ruffed grouse and grouse dogs induce such overt cir-
cumspection. Can or can't ruffed grouse be handled successfully by a
dog? If they can, then why so much egg-walking over which breed of
dog is best for the job? For those uninitiated in the vagaries of gunning
"Old Ruff," the questions would seem perfectly natural, logical. And,
even though the veterans of the grouse wars might cringe at such naiveté,
they should pause and remember their own earlier days of pristine innocence.

The king of game birds, the ruffed grouse is a combination of perversity, skittishness, and unpredictability. Here a cock grouse is seen "drumming," part of the annual spring mating ritual. Photo © Bill Marchel

The Nature of the Ruffed Grouse

In any event, deliberation of the subject of dogs for ruffed grouse hunting would be pointless before first examining the nature of the quarry itself. A hunter should know going in that he'll be confronting a creature so confounding as to defy definition. The only thing certain about grouse behavior is its very uncertainty. A combination of perversity, skittishness, and unpredictability, along with a near junglelike habitat, contributes mightily to the colossal stature of this drab gray or rufous-colored, medium-sized woodland bird—a bird aerodynamically deficient, whose enervating flush and erratic flight could rattle the nerves of a brain surgeon.

Unquestionably, the critter ornithologists label *Bonasa umbellus* is the most enigmatic of North America's game birds. One of the most consistently difficult aerial targets to bag, the grouse is unremittingly elusive, wary, tricky, flighty, and thoroughly inscrutable.

If you ever caught a ruffed grouse off guard, your hunting buddies would never believe you. The grouse's entire nervous system is seemingly tuned for danger. While other birds usually freeze instinctively when danger threatens, grouse often avoid trouble through an unhesitating, explosive aerial exit. Conversely, though, exasperating and unpredictable as the grouse is, he also might just flutter up into a handy evergreen and observe unnoticed as the intruder comes and goes.

But, then, too, he also might elect to hotfoot it over to some nearby cover, hunker down momentarily, only to flush noisily out the opposite side of the cover if the danger approaches too closely. Once in a blue moon, he'll comport himself as gentlemanly as a bobwhite quail, doggedly hugging the ground and rejecting flight virtually until booted from concealment. Just which tactic he'll choose at any given moment is guaranteed to keep gunners on guard.

Attempts to explain the grouse's baffling behavior link his deviant deportment with swings in barometric pressure, theorizing that imminent weather changes influence his sensitive nervous system and spark reactions to various environmental stimuli. Perhaps such scientific-sounding jargon intrigues the intellectually inclined, but it scarcely explains why a half dozen grouse flushed from similar covers within the same hour or so of the same day, can behave so differently. However, there is no question that certain weather conditions definitely affect grouse behavior. On windy days, they can be virtually unapproachable. Conversely, damp, still weather can effect the opposite reaction in the birds. But, whatever pulls his strings, the ruffed grouse, at best, must be viewed as a leery, moody, high-strung adversary, wily enough to often outwait, frequently outwit, and repeatedly outmaneuver a gunner, time after time after time.

Thus, when it comes to dog work, it should prove no great surprise that the ruffed grouse is no patsy. Sure, he can be handled by a dog . . . sometimes. But, remember, the dog always encounters the same capricious grouse behavior we hunters do. And, admittedly, a trio of dogless gunners can often kill more grouse than a pair of shooters hunting with an inexperienced or out-of-control dog.

I'm just as strongly convinced, however, that even a mediocre dog will produce better than a solo grouse gunner with no dog at all. Despite a likely lack of finesse or experience in handling the bird, the mere presence of a dog quartering ground around the gun suggests that the dog will move grouse the solitary hunter would bypass. If just a few of them flush toward or across the gunner, they'll present shots he might not get at straightaway birds he moves himself.

What Makes a Good Grouse Dog?

Practically any breed of gun dog will suffice for the lone grouse hunter. Among the flushing breeds, cockers, springers, or retrievers trained to quarter close can be effective both to push birds up and fetch those downed by the gun.

Traditionally, though, the term "grouse dog" is understood to mean one of the pointing breeds: dogs that hunt high-headed, their noses continuously questioning the air, seeking that cone of hot body scent that, when found, interrupts time and motion and forges dogs into statues. Nothing else can equal, much less surpass, the classic stance of an intense point on ruffed grouse.

Perhaps, the grouse's magic lies in the satisfying knowledge that the dog has accomplished no easy victory in finding, working, and pinning this hair-triggered bundle of perplexity and feathers. Or it is the rising anticipation of that explosive flush, of knowing it's coming but never sure exactly when? Whatever the reason, the point on grouse is always a thrill of the highest order.

This, then, is what separates simply hunting ruffed grouse with a dog from grouse hunting with a "grouse dog." Any pointing dog might, theoretically, be considered a potential grouse dog. In reality, only a small percentage ever qualify as more than middling to fair performers on grouse. And those few dogs that honestly merit being called "great" might be found only once in a lifetime.

As the saying goes, a good grouse dog is always born, never made. And giving truth to the maxim is the consensus that the truly exceptional grouse dog invariably seems endowed with an innate aptitude, a sort of extra-special sense for successfully handling these enigmatic birds. And while experience can only enhance the naturally great performer's work, it seldom improves the mediocre prospect's abilities. Grouse savvy

Success has smiled on this apparently dogless hunter—displaying the fan of a grouse tail—and his buddy. Hunting "Old Ruff" without a dog can be productive, but not as much fun, most gunners would agree. Photo © Denver Bryan

can't be infused; it only comes at conception.

Still, there are good grouse dogs of more moderate talent. The promising grouse dog must have a sensitive nose and the smarts to quickly learn how to use it efficiently. Once going on point, he must wait immobile for the arrival of the gunner and the subsequent flush. While hunting his quarry, he must perceptively work his ground and bird objectives, with a minimum of handling and frequently check in with his owner.

There are conflicting opinions on the grouse dog's most effective range and pace. One end of the spectrum prizes dogs that work slowly, deliberately, and always close to the gun. Diametrically opposed is the viewpoint that reveres dogs that work fast, with expanded range flexibility, reasoning that grouse hold tighter to a brisk approach and instant point than to a tentative pussyfooter.

Who's right? Which way is better, slow or fast? At various times and under differing conditions, I've seen dogs of both styles win the day. Then again, I've also seen hunts on which dogs of both styles failed badly, confirming my long held belief that no dog, even the greats, can handle grouse successfully every time out.

Despite all the head-shaking grief grouse can bestow on hunters and dogs, there are always a very, very few Elysian days when the birds seem glued to the ground and neither dog nor gunner can fall from grace. And it shouldn't matter that those times are rare. Were they routine, we'd value them less.

But those are the very days most highly prized by someone who hunts grouse with any dog, whether great, good, or just average. And whatever niche your dog occupies, there's always the hope that more than a few of these marvelously improbable birds will sometimes sit tight for his points.

* * *

So, having come full circle, there is a forthright answer to the question of whether grouse can really be hunted successfully with dogs. If success is measured by the sincere enjoyment, the genuine satisfaction you gain from a day afield with the gun dog you love—rather than from a bulging game pocket—the question begs no answer.

22

The Rearview Mirror:
Reviewing the Season Past

Season's end, whether it's the first or the umpteenth for you and your dog, signals the ideal time for a look in the rearview mirror—a review of your dog's field performance. With memories still vivid, such a review can go a long way toward determining what your future training thrust should be and setting your goals. Your objective assessment should concentrate not so much on *how much* game was collected, but rather, on *how your dog performed.*

In making that judgment, things to be pondered include your dog's working style (confident or tentative), scenting ability (sharp or unsure), handling responsiveness (crisply prompt or dilatory), marking and retrieving performance (accurate and gentle or inexact and hardmouthed), and general biddability (eager to please or overly independent). Clearly, there will be varying degrees in each of these categories.

Understandably, objectivity rarely comes easily when evaluating your dog—your pride and joy. Perhaps this is even more difficult for the first-time owner. I will try to help by providing this list of some of the most common problems gun dog owners face, along with a few practical solutions. It must be emphasized, however, that due to the diversity of problems occuring among the three major types of gun dogs, only a few examples can be cited.

RANGING TOO FAR AND TOO FAST

Spaniels and retrievers that flush (and to some extent, pointing breeds) that overextend their range can seriously mess up a hunt. A dog's fiery eagerness to find birds is too often to blame. In itself, this is more a

Check-cord work is one technique often used to correct overranging both in pointing breeds, like this German shorthair, and flushing dogs. Photo © Bill Buckley/The Green Agency

blessing than a fault. But when this eagerness results in consistent overranging, it usually indicates a lack of control on the owner's part, most likely due to insufficient or improper training to voice, whistle, and hand-signal commands.

The cure requires some check-cord training. A few sessions working the dog on a seventy-five-foot (23-m) check cord—turning him by whistle, voice, and hand signal each time he nears the end of the cord—should help eliminate the problem. Obviously, your dog must be well-versed in the meaning of your commands; rusty responses should prompt you to return to basic lessons once again.

Spaniels or retrievers used as flushing dogs should be made to HUP (SIT) on command whenever they exceed a range of about twenty-five yards (23 m) to either side or thirty yards (27 m) in front of the gun. Here again, your whistle command—one sharp blast—should make your dog plop his butt on the ground immediately.

A pointing dog can similarly benefit from check-cord and signal drills, although his range need not be as restricted as the flusher's. Encouraging both pointing and flushing dogs to hunt closer and work more deliberately can be accomplished by surreptitiously planting a few quail or pigeons close to you. Eventually, your dog should come to associate staying closer to you with finding birds. As a last resort, if your dog still consistently hunts too wide, you may have to try using one of the various range-reducing devices available commercially (See chapter 15, "Turning Fetchers into Flushers: Retrievers in the Uplands" for suggestions).

Ranging Too Close

The opposite, yet equally frustrating problem, is when your pointing dog always hunts too *close* to you. In that case, the dog is unlikely to find birds that you wouldn't stumble over yourself. If his hesitation to range out comes from an inclination to dawdle over old or nongame bird scent, you will probably need only get him into birds quicker and more often.

If too-stringent discipline is to blame, or the dog is just naturally overcautious, then you will have to cut him some slack and provide lots of encouragement to promote greater independence. Ordinarily, the quickest route to success will come from a temporary relaxation of discipline in the field, permitting the dog to bust and chase birds until his enthusiasm peaks again. A brief moratorium on shooting will often help hasten results as well, particularly if the dog's uneasiness is traceable to instances of heavy gunfire.

BREAKING POINT

It is not at all unusual for young dogs to break point, or merely to flash-point (a very brief hesitation), when their youthful eagerness and inexperience goad them into trying to catch birds themselves. Later, with maturity and increased hunting opportunities, the dog will learn that it's the gun that gets the birds.

But for now, you should encourage the dog to staunchly hold each successive point longer than the previous one. Start the training with some bobwhites, coturnix quail, or pigeons and a twenty-five- or thirty-foot (8- or 9-m) check cord. After you plant the birds (usually only two or three per session are recommended), work your dog into their vicinity. Then, when the dog goes on point, grab the check cord to make sure he doesn't break before you get to him. While you gently stroke the dog, put some moderate forward pressure on his hindquarters and tell him "Whoa" in a firm but soft voice. Note that the dog will counter that pressure and rigidly resist being pushed toward the bird. Continued regularly for a while, this little exercise will not only staunch but also lengthen the dog's points.

The follow-up phase should help the dog recognize and forge the connection between his holding a staunch point and the gun's function in getting the bird. The surest way to form this correlation is to shoot birds only over your dog's points and to ignore any wild flushes and deliberate or accidental bumps.

CROWDING BIRDS AND WHOA DEAFNESS

Whenever a pointing dog crowds birds and goes "whoa deaf"—ignores his owner's command to whoa—he becomes a distinct handicap to his owner by provoking premature flushes before the gun arrives. A serious fault, this is almost always the consequence of too much work on planted birds, which can be approached much more closely than wild ones, even without them dizzied.

Paradoxically, when sufficient work on wild birds is not possible, released or planted birds can often be used to help correct the problem. One method involves using pen-raised quail. Rather than hand-planting the quail, which usually leaves human scent on them, a better technique is "flight-planting."

First described in one of my earlier books, *The Practical Hunter's Dog Book*, flight-planting is the process of releasing quail out of gloved hands. The procedure enables the bird to take a relatively short flight before pitching into cover—simultaneously air-washing all or most human scent from it. Besides affording it a smell more like it would be in the wild, this method allows the bird to seek its own hiding place, thus leaving some helpful ground scent for the dog to work.

About ten minutes after the release, check-cord your dog near where you marked the bird down. At the very first sign that the dog has winded body scent, WHOA him and, if need be, reinforce your command with the check cord. At this time, it is imperative that you prevent any further attempts by the dog to move closer to the bird. Not even one step is permissible. Use the check cord as you firmly repeat the WHOA command, and make the dog stand fast for a full two minutes before the bird is flushed. Assuming the dog is not steady to wing and shot, having a helper to flush will make your job infinitely easier.

Be prepared to drill the dog on several successive outings to make sure the lesson becomes firmly entrenched. Should the dog continue crowding his birds, his prompt compliance to the WHOA command will help avoid the mistake whenever you catch him in the act.

Slow Fetching Return

Whether on land or from water, a retriever that dawdles in coming back to his owner with a downed bird can be very irritating. Every retrieve should be quick and decisive. Most often, the lethargic, hesitant return, owes to early handling mistakes, compounded by repetition.

Without realizing it, the overly impatient owner who tries to hurry a retrieve by going part way out to meet his returning dog, helps to reinforce the slow return. One way to alleviate the problem and speed up the retrieve is simply to turn and walk briskly away from the dog for a short distance. This usually encourages the dog to hurry so he can follow you. As your dog follows you, simply continue walking until he draws near, then turn to face him and accept the retrieve.

Harsh handling, too, may be at fault. If the dog pauses momentarily to shift his hold on the bird, or he accidentally drops it, and his owner gets on him too roughly, the dog may not be too eager to return

A speedy, direct retrieve to hand is what every waterfowl hunter should expect from his dog. This Lab wastes no time swimming back in with a mouthful of goose. Photo © Bill Marchel

a bird quickly. The solution is to take things a lot easier and try to keep a happy face on your outings, whether during training or actual hunting.

FAILURE TO TRAIL CRIPPLES

Waterfowl retrievers, more so than spaniels or pointing dogs, come up a bit short in the nose department, especially when it comes to trailing crips successfully. The reasons are many and varied.

Essentially, there's nothing wrong with the olfactory systems of field-bred retriever breeds. There are differences in individuals, of course, as in all breeds. These notwithstanding, however, I believe that most fetch dogs are trained according to field-trial standards, which rely primarily on using handler directions (mechanics) and very little on promoting independent scent searching.

Now, whether I'm right or wrong, the point here is to get around the problem of retrievers that fall short in successfully trailing and bringing back crippled birds. Forgetting field-trial niceties, you must encourage your retriever to use and rely on his nose. The earlier this is done, the better.

To achieve this will require laying some scent trails. Several methods can be employed. Shackled birds—ducks, pheasants, or pigeons whose wings are harnessed, strapped, or taped to their bodies—can be released to walk freely through various types of cover, thus laying a fresh scent trail that your retriever (or spaniel or pointer) is then encouraged to follow. Initially, the trails should be fairly short and easy to sort out. It is important that your dog cannot see the bird, so he'll be forced to use his nose to follow, find, and retrieve it. With proper progress, the scent trails can be made longer and more complex.

If live birds are not available, a scent drag can be used. A retrieving dummy, heavily soaked with commercial duck or game bird scent, is attached by a length of cord or sturdy monofilament line to a twelve- to fifteen-foot (3.5–4.5-m) bamboo pole. With the pole held at a right angle, the dummy is then dragged through the cover to form the scent trail. Sometimes, because the dog may pick up and follow his owner's trail rather than the scent drag, it's better to have someone else—preferably a stranger—lay the drag.

HARDMOUTH

When the game birds we hunt and admire are fetched back to us lacerated, disfigured, even crushed, we're understandably both offended and disappointed. Occasionally forgivable, a messy bird may be chalked up to canine retribution against an overly hostile cripple—a wing-tipped cock pheasant with ¾-inch (2-cm) spurs can inflict a Purple Heart–class wound on a poor dog trying to make an honest living. But, when regularity rears its ugly head, the problem of hardmouth flashes a not-to-be-ignored warning. Once begun, it never cures itself; it must be attacked posthaste.

If you can figure out what started hardmouth, a solution may suggest itself. If not, however, several procedures can be explored. One conventional method involves spiking dead game birds or pigeons with sections of stiff wire. Generally a half-dozen or so wires crisscrossed through the bird with their blunted points just barely protruding the skin. This practice, which is used in extremely difficult cases, isn't dan-

This yellow Lab exhibits a firm, gentle carry on a cock pheasant. Hardmouth should never be tolerated; once begun, it never cures itself. Photo © Mitch Kezar

gerous to the dog. When the dog first attempts to chomp the bird, he encounters the blunted wire immediately and softens his carry or drops the bird. If your dog drops the bird, he must be forced to hold the spiked bird for a minute or two. Obviously, if your dog hardmouths the bird, the blunted wires will make their own point! Generally, two or three more sessions will cause him to "lighten up."

A simpler technique that works well for curing milder cases, entails using a stiff, short-bristled hair brush with the handle removed. If your dog clamps down hard when fetching this type of brush, the bristles will prick his mouth, making the same point as a wired bird, just not as harshly.

Slightly frozen birds offer yet another approach to curing the problem. Bearing down on an icy cold exterior will chill the culprit's teeth, causing enough discomfort to generate a very soft, tender carry. Alternating the dog's retrieves between frigid and noniced birds—while working in a few spiked birds—should solve the problem over a few weeks' time. Even after the problem seems cured, however, making your dog retrieve an occasional "reminder" bird is good insurance against any recurrence of the problem.

THE HESITANT FLUSH

Considered a fault in spaniels by some, the tendency to pause briefly before moving in to flush a bird is thought by others to be an advantage. Sometimes the spaniel's hesitation to flush is prolonged into a flashpoint or even an actual point, much like that of a genuine pointing breed. Besides spaniels, some retrievers serving as flushing dogs also hesitate. In fact, today there are certain strains of Labradors bred specifically for their pointing proclivities.

Those spaniel owners who view the hesitant or "soft" flush as favorable say it provides the hunter a warning to get ready for action. Proponents of the bold or "hard" flush, which include field-trial participants, thrill to the decisive "get-airborne-or-lose-your-tail-feathers" hunting style. This is a question of personal preference, of course, but if you'd rather have your spaniel (or retriever) flush boldly and he is hesitant, there is a possible solution. As mentioned earlier in chapter 14, "Pigeons: Game Bird Substitutes," clipped-wing pigeons can be invaluable for promoting bold, aggressive flushing both in spaniels and retrievers.

This springer spaniel displays a bold, or "hard," flush to get a cock pheasant airborne. Many owners prefer this over the "soft" flush, that often resembles a flash-point, or even an actual point. Photo © Alan and Sandy Carey

Pulling or partially clipping a few primary feathers from one wing of a pigeon upsets the bird's flight equilibrium, making everything but short, erratic flights impossible. Therefore, these clipped-wing birds are relatively easy for a dog to catch, instilling in the dog the idea that boring in without hesitation enables him to grab that otherwise elusive, slippery customer; that is something he wants very much to do. After your dog catches birds for awhile and begins flushing boldly, wean him off the clipped-wings with some full-flighted pigeons. Should he hesitate, simply mix in a few "catchables" to get him back on track.

***

Certainly, the problems discussed here fall well short of a full roster of gun dog shortcomings. They are, however, the problems most commonly experienced by gun dog owners. If any have applied to your dog during the past season, waste no time in starting to correct them now. Not only will both you and your dog enjoy better hunting next fall, but your rearview mirror will also reveal a much brighter image at the end of next season.

These German shorthairs, who will divvy up the day's hunting, can be safely rested in secure car crates between turns afield. Photo © William H. Mullins

23

Setting Canine Goals
for the Coming Season

Just as looking back examines performance problems (see chapter 22, "The Rearview Mirror: Reviewing the Season Past"), looking forward offers you opportunity to improve your gun dog, as well as yourself. New Year's Day should claim no exclusive rights to making resolutions. In fact, for gun dog owners, the impending opening of hunting season far and away eclipses January 1 in importance. And plans to do some things differently this time around can prove a pivotal step toward more enjoyable and productive hunts for both you and your dog.

Resolving to provide as many opportunities as possible for your dog to hunt and come in contact with game is a good starting point. This is even more important if your dog is just going into his sophomore or junior year in the field. "What's so tough about a resolution like that?" you may ask. "Naturally, I plan on getting him out as much as I can." But wait a minute. How often, when you are joined by a buddy or two with their own dogs, have you voluntarily held your dog back, letting them send their more seasoned campaigners to hunt a special cover or tackle a difficult retrieve? More times than you care to recall? Without opportunities to gain experience and to make mistakes on game, your dog will not learn what's needed to be an effective gun dog.

Oh, sure, you drag out the usual excuse of wanting to prevent your young dog from screwing up the hunting for your friends. But maybe if you asked them, you would find that your buddies would be the first to insist on giving your dog the chance to succeed or fail, but above all, to learn. After all, they have certainly traveled that road before with their own dogs.

So, resolve to give your dog the learning experiences he deserves.

Discuss it openly beforehand with your gunning partners, and agree on evenly divvying up the work among all the dogs. Besides being fair, it's the most practical way to guarantee each dog gets adequate rest between hunting covers.

When hunting one dog at a time, you can leave one (or more) dogs back in your vehicle. A word of warning, though. Always make sure that the dogs left behind are safely and securely confined in separate crates. This insures that no dog fights will develop. Be absolutely certain, too, that the car is parked in a cool, shady spot, one that will remain shaded for however long you will be absent. All windows should be cracked at least an inch (3 cm) or so to provide adequate ventilation. And don't neglect to leave each dog some fresh water.

The anxiety over an inexperienced dog messing up your companions' shooting usually goes hand in hand with the worry of taking time out to correct a dog's miscues afield. Newer owners often agonize over any errors their dogs make, as errors may disparage the owner's capabilities as a trainer. Thus, they may feel that those mistakes, if merely overlooked, may be less obvious to others. But for the dog's own good, any shortlived embarrassment should be taken in stride and shrugged off in deference to the need for immediate correction of the dog's deliberate or inadvertent mistake. If your companions are themselves gun dog owners, they will surely expect you to call time to set your dog straight. And even if they're not dog people, after you explain the delay's importance to your dog's continuing field training, their forbearance should overcome any previous inclination toward impatience.

Heading into another gunning season, with its increased exercise levels, merits a closer look at your dog's diet. Resolve to replace his regular maintenance rations with additional protein and extra fat to provide him with the energy boost he'll need while working long, hard hours in the field. Balanced nutrition is almost universal among today's high-quality, commercial dry dog foods. According to many nutrition experts, supplementing dry dog food with meat is unnecessary. Yet, even when feeding a higher-protein dry food, adding a modest amount of meat to a dog's daily ration is, in my experience, advantageous during the hunting season. It appears to contribute an uptick in the verve and stamina needed for a dog to do a good job afield. And adding a few spoonfuls of meat to the meal will often tempt a weary dog to down his full ration, properly refueling himself for the next day's hunt.

Wearing a beeper collar, this English setter can easily be located by his owner, no matter how heavy the cover he hunts. Photo © Denver Bryan

If you can recall any occasion when your dog was out of sight and hearing distance last fall, you may resolve to try to eliminate the problem. But keeping track of an actively hunting gun dog isn't always easy. As locators, dog bells and hunter-orange collars team up well enough much of the time. But beeper collars have become increasingly popular for electronically keeping tabs on dogs. Infinitely more audible at longer distances than bells, the best of beepers can be programmed to let the hunter know whether his dog is moving or stopped on point. In the latter mode, the signal ceases briefly whenever the dog stops, then becomes audible again at a different tone and sequence while the dog remains on point, helping the gunner find his exact location.

There may be times during the season, though hopefully very few, when your dog strays beyond earshot of even a beeper. Whether running deer (a serious problem) or further exacerbating an overlong cast followed by a bumped bird and subsequent chase, if your dog is missing long and presumed lost, you'll experience that sickening sense of true panic. Before this happens, though, easing the worry and making your dog's safe return highly probable calls for another resolution. The first half of the resolution requires outfitting your dog with a collar ID tag or plate that includes not only your name, address, and phone number, but the word "Reward." Such an incentive is frequently enough to assure your dog's return.

The second half of the resolution—the real clincher—is having your dog permanently identified with an indelible tattoo. Various services and many veterinarians will tattoo your dog. Normally, placement is either on the dog's stomach or high on the inside of a thigh. Not only can a tatoo result in your *lost* dog being returned, but it virtually guarantees that he won't be *stolen*, in the first place, since most professional thieves look for such markings. Dog thieves generally sell their purloined canines to research laboratories, and, fortunately, most of those laboratories won't touch a tattooed dog.

These are only a few suggested resolutions to get you kick-started before next season arrives. Take that look forward, and you will probably come up with a handful of your own ideas to ensure a more successful, satisfying, and safe hunting season for you and your gun dog.

24

Lookin' Good:
Grooming Your Gun Dog

It is a mistaken belief of some owners that regularly grooming a gun dog is a waste of time. Sure, getting rid of tangled mats and sticktights in longhaired dogs after a day's hunt makes sense, they say. But, all that other fussing smacks of the fancy, show-dog set.

Nothing could be further from the truth. Regular grooming, which includes brushing, nail clipping, and minor barbering, is an important part of every gun dog's well-being, and the mark of a responsible, caring owner.

All hunting dogs, once properly conditioned to regular grooming, welcome these periodic sessions as extra opportunities to receive attention from their owners. Kennel dogs, who commonly get much less personal contact with, and affection from, their bosses than house dogs do, love to be groomed. And these sessions also give owners an ideal opportunity to check their dogs carefully for the beginning of any skin problems, eye irritations, ear infections, sores, cracked pads, and other assorted woes, which, if unnoticed and neglected may become more serious problems.

Grooming a kennel dog is best done in the basement of the house, on the porch, or in the garage. Any place other than the dog's kennel area offers a change of scenery and makes grooming a special occasion, giving the kennel dog an increased sense of belonging, while also breaking up the monotony of daily kennel living.

How often a gun dog should be groomed depends, to some extent, on his breed. Longhaired breeds, like the setters, spaniels, and goldens, require more coat care than the shorthaired breeds, such as Labradors and German shorthairs. Devoting five or ten minutes, at least three times

This owner removes burrs from his English setter's foot after the day's hunt. While post-hunt care is vital, regular grooming plays a beneficial part in your gun dog's normal routine. Photo © Kent and Donna Dannen

a week, to brisk brushings is ideal for the longhairs and isn't really over-doing it for any breed.

Most of the longcoated gun dogs get by nicely with a minimum of barbering, usually just a little strip-combing of the ears, as well as leg and tail feathering when the coat starts looking slightly scruffy. Electric clippers, used every few months, make quick work of cleaning up the neck and throat areas of setters and spaniels.

Just prior to hunting season, some hunters do a medium-length body clip on spaniels and setters. They will also eliminate virtually all of the leg feathering on both breeds and most of the tail feathering on the setters. As any owner of a longhaired gun dog knows, that attractive coat attracts more than admiration, especially after a day's hunting in moderately heavy cover. Burrs, stickers, twig bits, and weed seeds all seem to gravitate to it. While taking something away from the dogs' good looks, such barbering cuts down on the amount of field debris normally snagged in longhaired coats.

Besides a good trim, there is another way to avoid getting mementos of a day's work stuck in your dog's coat. Before the hunt, rub a light coating of baby oil—Johnson and Johnson's brand is ideal—into the body coat and feathering on your dog's legs and tail to ward off much of the bothersome debris. What does attach itself to an oiled coat combs out a lot more easily. In lieu of baby oil, some owners spray Pam, the no-stick cooking spray, lightly over their dogs' coats prior to starting out for the day. Both items are nontoxic and perfectly safe to use on your dog.

Nails on all gun dogs should be trimmed regularly to keep them at proper length and help avoid splitting or breaking. Generally, cutting nails back about every two to three weeks will suffice for dogs quartered indoors. Kennel dogs kept on cement runs usually wear their nails down and need only a periodic check to care for breaks or splits.

Besides the physical and psychological benefits regular grooming provides a gun dog, it should prove a matter of pride for every owner to keep his favorite hunting partner lookin' good!

Common household items can prove fatal to dogs, as well as kids. Keeping toxic substances out of reach of both species saves problems and, possibly, lives.
Photo © Bill Buckley/The Green Agency

25

Beware: Poisons

Like any accident, poisoning your gun dog shouldn't happen. But it does. All too frequently, dogs, curious creatures that they are, ingest poisonous substances thoughtlessly left around the home or garage.

Most parents of young children learn early to be scrupulously mindful of properly storing common household poisons, including bleaches, detergents, and medicines. Somehow, though, many folks tend to forget that dogs' curiosity makes them equally vulnerable to sampling toxic substances, often with fatal consequences.

For example, imagine you're doing some gardening chores in the front yard, refilling the sprayer with that stuff that raises hell with aphids when you notice a droopy rose bush. Momentarily setting down the open can of pesticide, you go to the garage for some fertilizer. "Tawny," your yellow Lab, who's been sunning herself on the front step, decides to investigate the odor coming from that container you left. Nuzzling it, she knocks it over and begins licking up the fluid. By the time you return and see what's happened, she's already showing distress signs. You race her to your vet . . . just barely in time to save her life.

Similar scenarios are repeated innumerable times throughout the year. In addition to pesticides, toxic agents usually found outside the home include antifreeze, paint thinner, herbicides, chemical fertilizers, solvents, and rodenticides.

Indoors, houseplants and medicines can also be dangerous. Among the popular houseplants with toxic properties for dogs are dieffenbachia, poinsettia, English ivy, calla lily, and mistletoe. Innocent, everyday medications commonly used by people, such as ibuprofen and acetaminophen, can be deadly to canines. So, too, is chocolate, if ingested in sufficient quantity.

Obviously, protecting your dog from exposure to the many toxic substances inside and outside your home is the best safeguard. Yet, accidents do happen. If you suspect your dog has been poisoned, speed is of the essence. Using a special hotline phone number, (800) 548-2423, you can contact the National Animal Poison Control Center (NAPCC) maintained by the University of Illinois College of Veterinary Medicine.

One of the NAPCC staff of licensed veterinarians will handle your call and provide advice on what to do when your dog ingests a specific poison. A member of the staff will also phone your own veterinarian for consultation on the problem. A fee of $30.00, charged to a major credit card (VISA, Mastercard, or AMEX), is assessed for each call, money well spent in such an emergency.

26

Dogs as Good Neighbors: A Considerate Owner Fosters Good Will

It is a pretty safe bet that a majority of gun dog owners share the dream—but not the reality—of a home centered in the privacy of hundreds of rolling acres of grassy fields and woodlots, preferably teeming with upland birds and waterfowl. More likely, those of us luckily removed from overcrowded urban centers, share the relatively close quarters of suburbia. Characterized by modesty of size, suburban lots, in most cases, abut neighboring parcels of comparable dimensions. Similar "estates" lie just across the road.

Albeit a pleasant environment, such a physical arrangement underscores the importance of maintaining peaceful coexistence. Aside from serious crime, the two primary causes of most neighborhood dissension unquestionably focus on rowdy young people and errant canines. Either group can easily earn a reputation as unredeemable, regardless of the magnitude of the misconduct or the impact on the neighborhood propriety. Dogs, in particular, engender a peculiarly selective attitude in many community residents. Even the smallest breach of canine decorum against thy neighbor can often scuttle a friendship or shatter a fragile pact of laissez faire.

The fact must be recognized that neighbors can indeed have legitimate gripes about our dogs; not all complaints are trivial and unjustified. Too many dog owners tend to be somewhat careless about their responsibilities, both to their animals and to the neighborhood in which they live.

It is pretty tough to ignore the aggravation caused by loose-running dogs in suburban communities. Whether through pure laziness or a just-don't-give-a-damn attitude, some owners casually slip their dogs

out the back door and foist them on the community, sometimes for the whole day or night. Obviously, left to their own devices, aimlessly wandering dogs will frequently destroy gardens, dig up lawns, upend garbage cans, constitute traffic hazards, and sometimes menace adults, kids, and even other dogs.

Besides allowing their dogs to run loose, suburban dog owners can often be guilty of other acts that set their dogs up as neighborhood nuisances. Topping the complaint hit parade, the habitually noisy dog; he begs neighbor alienation. The dog that ceaselessly yaps at everything— and nothing—whether housebound or outdoors, is guaranteed to frazzle the nerves of a saint.

If owners would only acknowledge the barking problem and tackle it head-on, correction is usually possible. There are various procedures to nip the barking habit in the bud. In my experience, the most efficient method yet devised employs an electronic bark collar. The best collars rely on delivering electronic stimulation immediately following several seconds of barking. These collars are available through most canine outlets and are relatively inexpensive.

Owners who permit their dogs, even though supervised, to romp freely in their own unfenced backyards are also toying with potential problems. Any dog not under reasonable control by his owner, even in the owner's yard, can become equally as bothersome as any other loose-running canine. Without benefit of a rope or lead, an uncontrolled dog is likely to exit his yard at the least provocation. Exhilarated by his sudden freedom, he's apt to barrel through any number of yards, leaving minor chaos in his wake. There go newly seeded lawns and freshly planted flower beds; and, as an extra bonus from his whirlwind visit, your dog may leave behind a fragrant memento. Also, to wind up his little spree, your dog could take to the streets and chase a car. And suppose the surprised driver abruptly swerves to avoid hitting the dog but then hits another motorist or, God forbid, a pedestrian. So much for unrestrained freedom without control.

All of this said, probably the most unpardonable thing a dog owner can do, either through consummate thoughtlessness or just plain stupidity, is unloosing a bitch in heat. Surely, such an act will reap a harvest

A howling English pointer won't make many points for his owner with the neighbors. Photo © Bill Buckley/The Green Agency

of unwanted puppies, which is unfortunate enough. But the worst aspect is the flood of canine suitors. Competing, often savagely, for the bitch's favor, these dogs can create a potentially dangerous situation for the hapless bystander.

Throughout her heat period, a bitch's owner must assume an extra measure of responsibility and keep her securely and safely confined. She should never be off a lead or rope during walks or exercise, and at such times, she should also be restricted to one small area. If necessary to take her away from home, physically carry her partway to avoid leaving an easily followed scent trail back to your house. Bothersome? Sure, but it is a responsible owner's twenty-one-day obligation to his bitch, as well as to his neighbors.

Another major source of inconsideration and potential trouble is a backyard kennel that's unattractively designed, poorly positioned, and slovenly maintained. Certainly, any sort of kennel that's unsanitary, smelly, and unsightly does nothing toward establishing good neighborly relations.

This kind of situation is easily preventable with a bit of thoughtful advanced planning. Carefully choosing an inconspicuous kennel site, one not in your neighbor's direct line of sight, is the first step. Then, artfully encircling it with some decorative evergreen shrubs as camouflage ensures the kennel run virtually escapes notice. Conscientious sanitation will keep it that way.

Typical suburban communities just naturally generate other potential pitfalls for dog owners. Specific circumstances may foster unique problems that either demand imaginative solutions or unusual efforts to circumvent. Gun dog owners in particular should be prepared to go the extra mile for the sake of their canines, which provide so much pleasure both as house pets and field companions. Our willingness as gun dog owners to go beyond the expected will help ensure an attitude of friendly acceptance for ourselves and our gun dog.

Here is a well-kept backyard kennel. It is whistle-clean, neat in overall ap-pearance, and certainly free from disagreeable odor. Photo © Jim Schlender

Will this chocolate Lab join his owner and family on their annual vacation, or become a candidate for a pet-sitting service, or go to a boarding kennel? Photo © Bill Buckley/The Green Agency

27

The Vacation Dilemma

Having given the company and the boss 110 percent productivity during some fifty-odd weeks since your last vacation, it is time again to delight in two weeks—maybe three, if *you're* the boss—free from the stress of the grind, while relaxing, sleeping in, fishing, golfing, swimming, or whatever. Well, almost whatever, considering that it's going to be a family vacation and parents and self-sacrifice are old acquaintances.

As a gun dog owner (hopefully not a brand-new one with an eight-week-old puppy [see chapter 4, "The How, When, Where, and Which of Pup Picking"]), vacation time involves both a decision and a responsibility. The former: whether your dog will accompany the family on vacation; the latter: ensuring that your dog will fare well, no matter what the verdict.

LEAVING YOUR GUN DOG BEHIND

Because it's the less-complicated choice, and, therefore, the most popular, consider vacationing without canine companionship. You have several options for your dog's daily care, feeding, and general well-being. Consigning the task to a friend, neighbor, or relative is one possibility. But, frankly, this is a lousy idea unless that caretaker intends to live in your house while you're away. Otherwise, too many things can go wrong with no one around to supervise the dog most of the time.

Dog- or pet-sitting services that offer daily care—which includes walking your dog (usually three times each day), feeding, and watering him, are available. Naturally though, without constant supervision, the same possibilities for problems exist with dog-sitting services as when friends or neighbors care for your dog. Live-in care is another option, and it, of course, offers the added security of house-watching.

The third option you have is leaving your gun dog's care in professional hands at a reputable boarding kennel. There, your dog will receive proper daily care and feeding, along with the assurance of comfort, safety, and, if it's needed, prompt medical attention.

Locating a reliable boarding facility reasonably near home shouldn't pose much of a problem, but it does deserve priority status well in advance of your vacation. During summer's most popular vacation weeks, it's not uncommon for first-rate boarding kennels to be booked solid months ahead of time. Without an early reservation, you could face boarding your dog in a more-distant or less-desirable establishment. To locate suitable, nearby facilities, consult your Yellow Pages, classified newspaper ads, specialty canine publications, dog-owning friends, and, last but not least, your own veterinarian, who himself may operate a boarding kennel.

With your top two boarding kennel choices targeted, make appointments at each for a personal visit and a brief but thorough, facility tour. Take careful note of the sanitation, making sure the quarters are clean and odor-free. Also make certain that your dog will be housed separately, in an inside kennel with a draft-free sleeping area, complete with fresh, clean, dry bedding. Kennel accommodations should open to an outdoor run that's roomy enough to allow exercise and the call of nature. The inside section should have adequate ventilation, while the outside run should provide ample shade.

Though wordless, the truest endorsement of a quality boarding operation will be reflected in the current canine occupants. If they don't appear clean, well fed and cared for, and, generally, seem less than animated and happy, make a graceful escape and hastily find another establishment.

Should the facility pass muster, however, all the other details and arrangements can then be finalized. Of primary concern will be the dates your dog will be boarded, the rates you'll be charged and, finally, seeing that whatever special instructions you may have about his daily care, diet, or medication, such as heartworm pills, are put in writing. Unless your dog's regular diet is the same type and brand of food used by the boarding kennel, you'll probably want to leave an adequate supply of rations.

There will probably be some rules you'll have to observe prior to leaving your dog at the facility. The management may require, for instance, that all your dog's shots be updated, including distemper, hepa-

An ideal boarding kennel will have well-maintained, scrupulously clean and comfortable separate runs, both indoors and outdoors. Photo © Jim Schlender

titis, leptospirosis, parvo, and rabies inoculations. Having all your dog's shots current is in your own best interest, too, since it safeguards your dog's health and well-being along with that of his fellow boarders.

When the Dog Must Come Along

Suppose you've decided—goaded unmercifully by the unified whimperings of kids and dog—that the family wouldn't be a family without "Old Faithful" along on vacation. In that case, get ready to organize lots of details well ahead of time. The first and most critical is making absolutely sure that the welcome mat will be out for guests with dogs at all of your stopovers, as well as your final destination.

Some motels that prohibit dogs in the rooms make a feeble attempt at accommodation by providing two or three austere kennel facilities. Meager at best, a motel kennel usually consists of short, narrow, fenced outdoor run with a too-small doghouse at the far end. Such Spartan quarters are bearable for a night or two, but scarcely suitable over an entire two-week vacation. Call ahead to find out what facilities are available.

Obviously, since dining will be part of the family vacation, an ample supply of your dog's regular food must be brought along, plus a little extra to meet any delay getting back home. You'll also need bowls for your dog's chow and water; a fork and tablespoon for scooping out and mixing canned meat and dry nuggets; his collar, complete with ID tag, license, and rabies tag attached; a lead; a twenty-five- to thirty-foot (7.5–9-m) rope or check cord for regulated exercise; a comb and brush; and a can of tick and flea spray. The first-aid kit you should normally carry in the car should serve to handle any minor canine mishaps that may occur on vacation. Looking ahead, if you're a well-versed car packer, your better half won't worry about reminding you to keep handy the dog's food, bowls, and other things you'll need while you're en route. And, naturally, you won't forget to fast the dog about six hours before starting your trip to avoid the possibility of carsickness.

In addition, how your dog rides in the car merits consideration. If he's ordinarily crated to and from the hunting field, then he won't mind similar travel accommodations while you're on vacation. No doubt, he'll be more comfortable in a crate to which he's accustomed, and he'll be safer, too. Crating your dog will also ensure your family's comfort and calm during the trip. In addition, your dog's crate will furnish a familiar place for him to bed down at night and even to be secured, if need be, while in your motel room or cottage.

Your vigilance will have to be doubled, considering that a strange vacation environment may adversely affect your dog's behavior. Courtesy toward other guests must be given high priority. You certainly don't want him to become a nuisance, barking excessively or running loose and soiling public areas. You cannot be careless while allowing him to take part in unaccustomed activities. Too frolicsome a dog, in a canoe with the kids, is an accident waiting to happen.

There's little room for doubt that vacationing with your gun dog involves substantial extra effort by the entire family. Still, the warm companionship, the amusing little traits, and the special fun that mark his presence more than compensate for the added inconvenience.

This English pointer seems to think he's in the driver's seat when it comes to accompanying the family on holiday. Even if he is going along, he'd be better off riding in his own crate. Photo © Bill Buckley/The Green Agency

A necessary milk break keeps these golden retriever pups and their Mom busily occupied. Photo © Henry H. Holdsworth

28

Breeding and the Joys of Parenthood

Just as strongly as the maternal instinct beats in the heart of most women, so the compulsion to produce a litter of puppies nags at the soul of most men who have ever owned a gun dog. It may lie dormant early on only to surface unexpectedly, all at once. Or, like a prowling lion, the desire may stealthily stalk the psyche, a step at a time, waiting patiently . . . to pounce!

Sudden or slow, once the notion enters your mind, capitulation is inevitable. If the owner's would-be parent is male, the road to meaningful romance bodes a rocky trip at best. Females, on the other hand, hold infinitely greater promise of "marrying well." The idea of a bitch whelping a litter of pups, some or all of which may grow up to greatness, could put a smile of anticipation on the face of a gargoyle. And, though the bottom line may differ among owners, the typical goal is to secure a pup as good as Mom.

But what are the odds of propagating a litter to duplicate their dam's quality, much less surpass it? Astronomically poor, indeed, if you merely settle for breeding your bitch to whatever male of the same breed happens to be conveniently at hand. Snap decisions based on expedience or hunches seldom produce worthwhile results in animal husbandry. Good breeding demands some thoughtful planning and research to formulate a suitable match. That doesn't mean you have to be an expert, though, to grasp the essentials of good breeding and avoid commonly made mistakes. The following are among the major factors you should consider before deciding to breed your bitch.

Careful selection of a prospective sire should head the list. The stud dog you choose should be as fault-free as possible. Since perfection is never attainable—only sought after—no stud dog will be totally flawless. But the fewer faults he has, the better, and those few must be iden-

The carefully chosen sire of your gun dog "kids" should demonstrate keen hunting instincts along with proper physical conformation and stable temperament and intelligence. Photo © Denver Bryan

tified at the outset.

Look for such physical faults as substandard conformation, straight shoulders, swayback (excessive downward curvature of the spine), roachback (a convex curvature of the spine near the loin), poor tail carriage, under- or oversized body frames, cowhocks (when the hocks turn in toward each other), splayfootedness, and under- or overshot jaw.

These are the easy-to-spot imperfections. Your much tougher assignment is uncovering the hidden flaws, the ones not immediately detectable to the eye. Things like temperament and intelligence are qualities even more critical than certain physical traits in a prospective sire. A minor physical defect or two may easily be dismissed, but a stud dog found wanting in intelligence or good temperament should be instantly eliminated from consideration.

Secondly, keep in mind one of the major no-nos: two dogs with the same faults should never be bred to each other. Just as breeding dogs that possess analogous good qualities intensifies those desirable traits, it likewise holds true that any shared defects will also be intensified by breeding. Consequently, you must be as hard-nosed in evaluating your bitch's faults as you are in checking out a prospective stud.

Of course, before you can form any final appraisals about the papa you'd like for your gun dog "kids," you'll have to check around for prize catches. You may find just what you want close to home, possibly among your buddies' dogs. More likely, your search will focus on advertised stud dogs, those with documentation of prepotency in producing exceptional puppies. Virtually without exception, these proven sires will be established field-trial competitors with demonstrable pass-along talents as seen in the numbers of their own trial wins and those of their progeny. Though a litter of potential field-trial winners may be the farthest thing from your mind, a stud dog's record of field-trial wins, plus those of the pups he's sired, offers tangible evidence of the stud's hunting abilities, as well as his effectiveness in endowing his offspring with those valued attributes.

Not every field-trial winner or champion will fit your requirements. If your bitch is a close-working pointing dog, for instance, and that's what you want to replicate in her pups, don't consider an All-Age Stakes stud that consistently sires big-running progeny. Instead, focus on a winner of shooting dog and/or Shoot-to-Retrieve stakes whose range should be much more compatible with that of your bitch. Strive to match as closely as possible the type of hunting style and performance you'd like to see in your pups with that displayed in the achievements of the prospective stud dog.

Unfortunately, a dog lacking field-trial placements offers little up-front information about his own hunting qualifications, much less the field capabilities of pups he's sired. And, short of hunting over him or them yourself, or accepting a favorable consensus from others who have, there's not much to go on besides pedigree.

A valid information instrument, the pedigree is a certified record of the stud dog's ancestry—literally, a dog's family tree. Like any family tree, a dog's pedigree lists the names of his close and distant relatives, depending on the number of generations it covers. Usually of more significance, though, are the various titles that go with those names. In the form of prefix abbreviations (see appendix for meanings), they testify to each dog's achievements.

Knowledgeably read, a pedigree indicates to you just how many ancestors are traced from field breeding or bench show bloodlines. Too large a percentage of the latter indicates that the natural hunting potential that the stud dog can pass on to his pups will probably be seriously diminished. Carefully and understandably employed, a pedigree provides the most dependable device for comparing the bloodlines of your bitch with those of the prospective sire. Normally, the more close relatives they share, the more likely the uniformity of the puppies produced. And this is the underpinning of good breeding.

Taking the necessary research into account, the decision to breed your bitch should be made well in advance of her next heat. Planning ahead a full six months would be none too early. You can start the project when your bitch comes into heat, so all arrangements will be in readiness to coincide with her next expected heat period, six months later.

Make certain, once your sire-to-be has been determined, that all arrangements are well defined, agreed upon in writing, and signed by both parties. At that point, also find out where to ship or bring your bitch and verify the exact day in her heat period that she should be available at the stud dog's kennel. Usually the twelfth day is considered opitimum for conception, but it does vary with individual bitches. It is also common practice for a stud to service a bitch more than once, sometimes on the eleventh, twelfth, and thirteenth days.

Many failures to conceive after stud service trace to problems that can be easily recognized by a veterinarian during a prebreeding examination. Therefore, about a month before your bitch is due in heat, you should schedule a thorough veterinary examination to make sure she's healthy and in good condition to be bred.

After breeding, when she is safely back home, your little girl must be kept under wraps, secure from additional male companionship, for the rest of her heat period. For another three weeks, continue her routine diet. At the start of the fourth week, however, she should begin receiving additional amounts, supplemented with vitamins and calcium as prescribed by your veterinarian. Normal exercise should continue regularly for the first three weeks of her pregnancy. During the following six weeks, carefully monitor all exercise, with no strenuous activity at all in the last three weeks.

Although nine weeks (sixty-three days) is the normal gestation period for dogs, D-day (D for delivery, of course) can vary by two or

Usually, whelping occurs naturally and without incident. This black Labrador bitch whelped her litter in a couple of hours and has given her pups the tender, loving care they deserve. Soon, the proud owner will face the daunting task of selecting one pup to keep. Photo © Lon E. Lauber

three days either way. Having preselected an appropriate, quiet, warm, draft-free place for delivery, you should set up a suitable whelping box. This is generally a wooden box with a floor and sides but no top, large enough for the bitch to sleep in comfortably while stretched out on her side. The sides of the whelping box must be low enough to permit the bitch easy access, but sufficiently high to keep puppies inside for several weeks. Guard rails, mounted about five or six inches (13 or 15 cm) above the floor on all four sides and approximately four inches (10 cm) out from each side, keep any pups that squirm between the bitch and the sides from being accidentally crushed. Allow your bitch time to become used to the whelping box. Let her have free access to it, even sleep there if she chooses, for four or five days. This will help relieve her natural uneasiness and make whelping more comfortable for her.

Usually, whelping occurs quite naturally and without difficulty or incident. Although it can sometimes stretch up to ten or twelve hours, depending on the individual bitch and the litter size, it ordinarily takes less than two hours.

As soon as possible after whelping is complete, the newborns must start nursing. This is when they obtain the colostrum in the bitch's milk, making them temporarily immune to disease.

Now, with your six . . . or seven . . . or eight pups contentedly nursing, all warm and secure with their mom, you can heave a sigh of relief and "parental" pride. A moment of satisfaction is called for before you embark on two months or more of near nonstop attention, cleanup, scrutiny, feeding, scrutiny, socializing, scrutiny, decision, advertising, and finally, scrutiny—this time of would-be foster parents.

Appendix 1

SOURCES FOR MORE IMFORMATION
When requesting information from any of these groups, always include a self-addressed, stamped envelope.

Health Organizations
Canine Eye Registration Foundation (CERF), Purdue University, 1248 Lynn Hall, West LaFayette, IN 47907
National Animal Poison Control Center Hotline (800) 548-2423
Orthopedic Foundation for Animals (OFA), University of Missouri-Columbia, 2300 E. Nifong Blvd., Columbia, MO 65201-3856

Breed Registries
American Kennel Club, 5580 Centerview Dr., Raleigh, NC 27606
    Note: This address is for registration only. For all other matters, write the AKC at 51 Madison Ave., New York, NY 10038
Field Dog Stud Book, American Field Publishing Co., 542 S. Dearborn St., Chicago, IL 60605-1598
United Kennel Club, 100 E. Kilgore Rd., Kalamazoo, MI 49001

Field Trial and Hunt Testing Organizations
American Kennel Club, 51 Madison Ave., New York, NY 10038
American Bird Hunter's Association, Charles Adams, secretary, 510 E. Davis Field Rd., Muskogee, OK 74401
The American Field, 542 S. Dearborn St., Chicago, IL 60605-1598
National Bird Hunter's Association, Stan Wint, secretary, 14200 Waverly Rd., Gardner, KS 66030
National Shoot-To-Retrieve Association, Bob Cunningham, president, 226 N. Mill St., Suite 2, Plainfield, IN 46168
North American Hunting Retriever Association, P.O. Box 1590, Stafford, VA 22555
North American Versatile Hunting Dog Association, Bob Hauser, 395 County Rd. 900E, Tolono, IL 61880

Gun Dog Periodicals
The American Brittany, P.O. Box 616, Marshfield, MO 65706
The American Field, 542 S. Dearborn St., Chicago, IL 60605-1598
The American Water Spaniel Club Newsletter, 18515 Lake George Blvd. NW, Anoka, MN 55303

Bird Dog News, 563 17th Ave. NW, New Brighton, MN 55112

The German Shorthaired Pointer News, 86 N. Heck Hill Rd., P.O. Box 850, St. Paris, OH 43072

GSPCA Shorthair, German Shorthaired Pointer Club of America, 18151 Harrison St., Omaha, NE 68136

Gun Dog Magazine, P.O. Box 35098, Des Moines, IA 50315

Gun Dog Supreme, Richard Bovard, ed., 2820 Edgewood Dr. N., Fargo, ND 58102

Pointing Dog Journal, P.O. Box 968, Traverse City, MI 49685

Retriever Journal, P.O. Box 968, Traverse City, MI 49685

Retriever Field Trial News, 4213 S. Howell Ave., Milwaukee, WI 53207-5095

Spaniels In The Field, 10714 Escondido Dr., Cincinnati, OH 45249

Pamphlets & Booklets

Major manufacturers of dog foods and pet supplies offer literature covering an array of subjects of interest and importance to gun dog owners. The bulk of these materials is free, though a nominal fee may be required for some items. Send a written request and a self-addressed, stamped envelope for a list of available publications.

Agway, Inc., 333 Butternut Dr., DeWitt, NY 13214

Best Feed & Farm Supplies, Inc., P.O. Box 246, Oakdale, PA 15071

Friskies Pet Care Co./Alpo Pet Foods, Inc., 800 N. Brand Blvd., Glendale, CA 91203

Hartz Mountain Corp., Frank E. Rogers Blvd. S., Harrison, NJ 07029

Iams Co., 7250 Poe Ave., Dayton, OH 45414

Kal Kan Foods, Inc., 3250 E. 44th St., Los Angeles, CA 90058

Quaker Professional Services, 585 Hawthorne Ct., Galesburg, IL 61401

Ralston Purina Co., Checkerboard Sq., St. Louis, MO 63164-0001

Insurance

Veterinary Pet Insurance (DVM/VPI), 4175 E. LaPalma Ave. #100, Anaheim, CA 92807-9903

Tattoo Registry

National Dog Registry, P.O. Box 116, Woodstock, NY 12498

Tattoo-A-Pet, 6571 SW 20th Ct., Ft. Lauderdale, FL 33317

Other Organizations

American Boarding Kennels Association, 4575 Galley Rd., Suite 400-A, Colorado Springs, CO 80915

American Animal Hospital Association, P.O. Box 150899, Denver, CO 80215-0899

American Veterinary Medical Association, 1931 N. Meacham Rd., Schaumburg, IL 60173-4360

North American Game Bird Association, Attn: John Mullin, P.O. Box 96, Goose Lake, IA 52750

Pet Food Institute, 1200 19th St. NW, Washington, DC 20036

Appendix 2

GUN DOG TRAINING EQUIPMENT, ACCESSORIES, AND SPECIAL ITEMS

Where to locate needed gun dog items can often puzzle new gun dog owners. Frequently, canine supply catalogs offer the products not easily found elsewhere. Listed below are some of the major firms catering to gun dog owners

Dog Crates and Station Wagon Barriers
Doskocil, P.O. Box 1246, Arlington, TX 76004-1246
Kennel-Aire Mfg. Company, 6651 Hwy. 7, St. Louis Park, MN 55426

Dog Boxes for Pickup Trucks
Creative Sports Supply, P.O. Box 765, Attalla, AL 35954
Rose Metal Products, P.O. Box 3238, Springfield, MO 65808
Quality Dog Box and Trailers Co., Rt. 1, Box 94A, Weleetka, OK 74880

Kennel Fencing and Panels
Bob Long Kennel Runs, Box 187, Gambrills, MD 21054
Mason Fence Company, 260 Depot St., P.O. Box 365, Leesburg, OH 45135
Horst Company, 101 E. 18th St., Greeley, CO 80631

Dog Houses
Dogloo Company, 6817 N. 22nd Place, Phoenix, AZ 85016
Drake Design, Inc., 1700 Oak St., Kansas City, MO 64108

General
Dogs Unlimited, Box 1844, Chillicothe, OH 45601
Drs. Foster & Smith, Inc., 2253 Air Park Rd., Rhinelander, WI 54501
Dunn's Supply Store, P.O. Box 449, Grand Junction, TN 38039
Gun Dog Supply, 626 Ridgewood Rd., Ridgeland, MS 39158

Happy Jack, Box 475, Snow Hill, NC 28580
Hulme Sporting Goods, & Mfg. Co., Box 670, Paris, TN 38242
J-B Wholesale Pet Supplies, 5 Raritan Rd., Oakland, NJ 07436
Nite Lite Company, P.O. Box 8210, Little Rock, AR 72221
Scott's Dog Supply, 9252 Crawfordsville Rd., Indianapolis, IN 46234
Tidewater Specialties, U.S. Rt. 50, Wye Mills, MD 21679
Valley Vet Supply, East Hwy. 36, P.O. Box 504, Marysville, KS 66508

Appendix 3

TITLES OF ACHIEVEMENT

Pedigrees show each individual ancestor in the dog's lineage, the dog's registration number plus any titles won, and, depending on registry, Orthopedic Foundation for Animals (OFA), and Canine Eye Registration Foundation (CERF) certifications. Titles won in competitive events normally appear as prefixes; others as suffixes. Breeders will always take the time to explain what the numerous titles on a pedigree mean. However, the ones of major significance to the hunter follow below.

AFC, AFTC, Am. Fld.Ch.: The title indicates a dog has won an Amateur Field Trial Championship.

CD: Companion Dog. A basic Obedience Trials title.

CDX: Companion Dog Excellent, a higher level in Obedience Trials. Neither of these two titles demonstrates a dog's field capabilities.

Ch.: An American Kennel Club (AKC) title bestowed in dog show competition. Beware of too many of these in a pedigree.

DUAL Ch.: Stands for Dual Champion, a dog that has won both in the field and on the bench. Same caution holds true as for the Ch. title above.

FTC, FC, Fld.Ch.: A Field Trial Champion.

Glossary

American Field Publishing Co.: Publishes *The American Field*, a weekly newspaper devoted to pointing dog field trial reports and other items of interest. Also maintains *The Field Dog Stud Book*, which registers purebred dogs.

American Kennel Club (AKC): The nation's largest purebred dog registry, the AKC registers all breeds it recognizes. Also regulates dog shows, hunting tests, field trials, etc.

bench: A bench or cubicle for dogs entered in a "benched" dog show; also a kind of synonym for dogs of show bloodlines, *i.e.*, "bench bred."

bitch: A female canine.

bump a bird: A pointing dog is said to bump a bird he flushes accidentally, as opposed to busting a bird, which is a willful, deliberate flush.

call name: The short name given a dog for everyday use, such as Fido, Rover, etc.

champion: The title given a dog that has won a championship event, such as a dog show or field trial.

cow-hocked: A condition wherein the dog's hocks turn in toward each other.

crossbreeding: Mating dogs of different breeds.

dam: The female parent.

dock: A shortening of the dog's tail by cutting; thus, dock-tailed.

dog: The male canine.

drag: The scent trail left by dragging a scent-impregnated bag along the ground for training purposes.

***Field Dog Stud Book*:** The registry maintained by The American Field Publishing Co.; used primarily for the registration of purebred hunting breeds.

field-bred: Dogs from field (hunting) lineage at least several generations in succession.

field trial: A competitive event for hunting dogs. There are separate trials for each of the major types of gun dogs, *i.e.*, retriever, spaniel, and pointing dog. Field trials are also held for various breeds and types of hounds.

flash point: An abbreviated, momentary point before a dog breaks to bust a bird. Normally associated with young, over-enthusiastic pointing dogs.

flight-planting: The technique of releasing pen-raised game birds either from gloved hands or directly from a pen to eliminate as much human scent as possible. The method helps create a more realistic situation for dog training.

flush: The act of forcing a bird to take flight from cover.

flushing dog: Dogs used to find and flush game birds for the gun.

hardmouth: Describes a dog that chomps or chews the birds he retrieves.

heat: The semiannual period of the bitch.

gun: A term used to designate the hunter, the gunner, or the gun itself.

gun-shy: The condition of fear or nervousness a dog exhibits at the sound, or, sometimes the sight, of a gun.

inbreeding: The mating of closely related dogs of the same breed.

interbreeding: The mating of dogs of different strains or varieties.

line breeding: The mating of dogs within a line or family to a common ancestor, such as grandson to granddam or granddaughter to grandfather.

official name: Generally, the registration name given a dog.

outcrossing: The breeding of unrelated dogs of the same breed.

overshot jaw: When the front teeth of the upper jaw overlap those of the lower jaw in the closed-mouth position.

pedigree: The written record of a dog's ancestry for three or more generations.

quartering pattern: The pattern adapted by the gun dog as he ranges to the front and swings from left to right of the hunter, similar to a windshield wiper.

roachback: A convex curvature of the back near the loins.

roading harness: A special harness designed to provide pulling exercise for the dog, used to strengthen legs and chest muscles and provide aerobic benefit.

scent trail: Literally, the trail of scent left on grass, vegetation, brush, and the ground where a bird walked. Also an artificially produced trail laid by a scent drag, for training purposes.

sire: The dog (male) that fathers a litter.

splayfoot: A flat foot from which the toes spread.

steady to wing and shot: When a pointing dog remains immobile on point, throughout the flush of the bird and the firing of the gun, until released to continue hunting. In waterfowl hunting, retrievers are merely steady to shot, *i.e.*, remaining seated in or near a blind until ordered to fetch a downed duck or goose.

strip-combing: A grooming process for longhaired breeds using a special utensil containing a razor blade, which thins the coat, leaving a natural, uncut appearance.

stud book: A registry or record of the breeding details of various recognized breeds.

swayback: A concave curvature of the back, from withers to hipbones.

trail: When a dog hunts by following ground scent.

training table: Literally, a table, with up and down ramps, on which dogs are trained. A training table brings the dog up closer to the trainer, incorporating the psychological aspect of a dog's insecurity at being off the ground, therefore making him more dependent on and attentive to his trainer.

undershot jaw: When the front teeth of the lower jaw protrude beyond the front teeth of the upper jaw in the closed mouth position.

WHOA: The command used to make the pointing dog stop instantly and remain so until released.

whoa deaf: When a pointing dog willfully ignores a WHOA command.

Suggested Reading

Whether a first-time gun dog owner or an experienced hand, additional information about your own favorite breed (as well as others); about new or unusual training procedures; and about various philosophies, advice, tips, and equipment will always prove of interest and add to your overall understanding of gun dogs. In addition to the information available from the sources listed in Appendix 1, such valuable and diverse information can be found in the following books.

Pointing Dogs
Bailey, Joan. *How to Help Gun Dogs Train Themselves,* 2nd ed. (Hillsboro, OR: Swan Valley Press, 1993).

Evans, George Bird. *Troubles With Bird Dogs, and What to Do About Them: Training Experiences with Actual Dogs Under the Gun.* (Piscataway, NJ: Winchester Press, 1975).

Falk, John R. *The Complete Guide to Bird Dog Training,* rev. ed. (New York: Lyons & Burford, 1994).

Long, Paul. *Training Pointing Dogs: All The Answers To All Your Questions,* rev. ed. (New York: Lyons & Burford, 1985).

Robinson, Jerome B. *Hunt Close: A Realistic Guide to Training Close-Working Gun Dogs for Today's Tight Cover Conditions.* (New York: Winchester Press, 1978).

Roebuck, Kenneth C. *Gun Dog Training: Pointing Dogs.* (Mechanicsburg, PA: Stackpole Books, 1983).

Wehle, Robert G. *Wing & Shot.* (New York: Country Press, 1964).

West, Bob. *Basic Gun Dog Training (and Then Some).* (Des Moines, IA: Stover Publishing Co., 1993).

Flushing Dogs
Goodall, Charles S., and Julia Gasow. *The New English Springer Spaniel,* 3rd ed. (New York: Howell Book House, 1984).

Irving, Joe. *Training Spaniels.* (Shrewsbury, England: Swan Hill Press, 1993).

Pfaffenberger, Clarence J. *Training Your Spaniel,* rev. ed. (New York: Howell Book House, 1963).

Roebuck, Kenneth C. *Gun-Dog Training Spaniels And Retrievers.* (Mechanicsburg, PA: Stackpole Books, 1982).

Spencer, James B. *HUP! Training Flushing Spaniels the American Way.* (New York: Howell Book House, 1992).

Retrievers

Free, James L. *Training Your Retriever,* 3rd ed. (New York: Coward-McCann, 1968).

Milner, Robert, and Lawrence McHugh. *Retriever Training for the Duck Hunter.* (Grand Junction, TN: Junction Press, 1985).

Quinn, Tom. *The Working Retrievers: The Training, Care, and Handling of Retrievers for Hunting and Field Trials.* (New York: E.P. Dutton, 1983).

Robinson, Jerome B. *Training The Hunting Retriever.* (Canaan, NH: J.B. Robinson, 1987).

Tarrant, Bill. *Hey Pup, Fetch It Up!: The Complete Retriever Training Book,* (Mechanicsburg, PA: Stackpole Books, 1993).

Wolters, Richard A. *Game Dog: The Hunter's Retriever for Upland Birds and Waterfowl: A Concise New Training Method.* (New York: E.P. Dutton, 1983).

————. *Water Dog: Revolutionary Rapid Training Method.* (New York: E.P. Dutton, 1964).

General Gun Dog Titles

Bamberger, Michelle. *Help! The Quick Guide to First Aid For Your Dog.* (New York: Howell Book House, 1993).

Duffey, David M. *Hunting Dog Know-How,* rev. ed. (Piscataway, NJ: Winchester Press, 1983).

————. *Expert Advice on Gun Dog Training,* rev. ed. (Piscataway, NJ: Winchester Press, 1985).

Falk, John R. *The Practical Hunter's Dog Book,* rev. ed. (Stillwater, MN: Voyageur Press, 1991).

Fergus, C. *Gun Dog Breeds, A Guide to Spaniels, Retrievers, and Pointing Dogs.* (New York: Lyons & Burford, 1992).

Tarrant, Bill. *Gun Dog Training: New Strategies from Today's Top Trainers.* (Stillwater, MN: Voyageur Press, 1996).

Walkowicz, Chris, and Bonnie Wilcox. *Successful Dog Breeding: The Complete Handbook on Canine Midwifery,* 2nd ed. (New York: Howell Book House, 1994).

Index

About the Author

John R. Falk has authored three books on dogs (*The Practical Hunter's Dog Book*, published by Voyageur Press; *The Complete Guide to Bird Dog Training;* and *The Young Sportsman's Guide to Dogs*). His numerous magazine articles on gun dogs, shooting, hunting, and fishing subjects have appeared in *Sports Afield, Field & Stream, North American Hunter, Mechanix Illustrated, Ducks Unlimited,* and *American Sportsman,* among others. John served for eleven years as gun dog editor of *Guns and Hunting* magazine, for nine years in similar capacity for *The American Shotgunner* magazine, and for ten years as gun dog editor of *Shooting Sportsman* magazine. The former public relations manager of Olin Corporation's Winchester Division, John has hunted extensively in the United States, Canada, Mexico, and Central and South America, as well as in Italy. He lives in South Salem, NY, with his wife, and he has one son.

English setters "Star" (left) and "Brooke" seen here with their best friend, author John R. Falk.